Microeconomics

Microeconomics

A Computational Approach

Gerald E. Thompson

M.E. Sharpe
Armonk, New York
London, England

Library of Congress Cataloging-in-Publication Data

Thompson, Gerald E.
    Microeconomics : a computational approach / Gerald E. Thompson.
        p. cm.
    Includes index.
    ISBN 0-7656-0664-X (alk. paper)
        1. Microeconomics—Mathematical models. 2. Linear programming. 3. Decision
making. 4. Mathematical optimization. 5. Econometric models. I. Title.

HB172.T59 2001
338.5′01′51—dc21   00-032977

Printed in the United States of America

BM (c)   10   9   8   7   6   5   4   3   2   1

Contents

List of Diagrams, Figures, Tables, and Policy Boxes

Diagrams

Figures

Tables

Policy Boxes

Preface

In dealing with the real problems that confront us, there is the desire to be able to handle in a reasonable way the many alternative courses of action, the uncertainty, and the many restraining influences—some due to scarce resources, some due to institutional practice and policy, and some due to minimum or maximum limits placed upon particular activities (e.g., minimum levels of service or quality and maximum levels of undesirable side effects). In large part the work ahead for us will involve participation (perhaps indirectly) in the planning of activities under these conditions; some will be in profit-oriented firms and some in public or quasi-public units such as government agencies, regulated enterprises, health and educational institutions, and the like.

What we have now in linear programming and decision analysis, together with traditional analysis, are ways of studying microeconomic problems that better prepare us for work in the various areas of interest. It is our good fortune at this point to have a variety of models, procedures, and approaches, together with strong computational assistance, that aids us greatly in our quest to understand, to predict, and to guide economic activities.

There is still much to be done, however, in achieving a greater familiarity with various aspects of some of the more recent models. Such models can be quite useful in representing and studying a segment of reality that is of interest to us, but it is only through a familiarity with all the major models that it becomes possible to select the one that best fits the circumstances and also best serves our purposes.

One of the important roles of economic theory and models is that of providing a framework through which reality may be viewed, interpreted, predicted, and perhaps influenced. Models and theories provide some "tracks" that guide us in thinking about reality. Thus, models have an influence far beyond providing solutions to specific problems, important as that might be. They also guide and prod our minds in subtle and significant ways as we make intuitive judgments and choices.

The traditional models, using the methods of the calculus, provide us with the familiar smooth curves and permit, for example, the determination (in the model at least) of equilibrium levels of output for the firm (and equilibrium levels of consumption for the consumer) by identifying points of tangency or other slope conditions. In short, they involve the optimization of the calculus.

In contrast, linear programming provides an optimization procedure using only the algebra associated with linear equations and linear inequalities. The smooth curves are replaced by linear or piecewise linear graphs. Equilibrium (optimal) levels (of output, for example) are obtained by identification of points of intersection of linear or piecewise linear graphs.

A linear programming model, compared to the usual traditional model, can be a far simpler model of a given segment of reality. One should not judge the value of the model, however, solely by applications where such rough approximations are made. It must also be noted that in the linear programming model, it is very easy to make the piecewise linear segments shorter and shorter so that the smooth curves of the calculus model are essentially obtained. Solutions to the piecewise linear model are obtained by the same simple optimization procedure as that used in the simple linear programming model involving a very rough approximation to the real solution.

This is a point that does not seem to be fully realized. There exists now a powerful optimization procedure relevant to virtually all aspects of economics that does not require great mathematical preparation in order to solve optimization problems. Access to modern computational facilities is necessary, of course, to solve large practical problems. To be sure, more than a minimal amount of mathematical preparation is desirable, and skilled professionals in the field should be fully trained in both the traditional calculus optimization procedures and the linear programming optimization procedures. But for many people a choice of emphasis in their training must be made. It seems rather clear that when there is a low limit on the time available for training and when a need for effective skill in undertaking optimization studies exists, learning the linear programming procedures should have the higher priority. And the closer one gets to real-world problems, the more important the advantages of the linear programming procedures become.

One of the important characteristics of linear programming procedures is the way in which the thinking about problems in terms of models is facilitated. First, it can easily be seen that models can provide predictions or solutions for real-world problems that otherwise would not be available. Second, linear programming models generate strong motivation and early reinforcement in the study of models because problems of some interest can be solved after quite limited study. By obtaining graphical solutions to meaningful problems, a view is obtained of the need for procedures to solve the larger real problems characterized by numerous resource inputs and numerous product outputs and processes. Third, moving on to the algebra-based procedures does not involve big steps. The simple algebraic procedures can be illustrated in terms of the small problems that were solved graphically.

This transition from a small problem that can be graphed to larger problems that cannot be graphed is far easier in linear programming than in the traditional procedure. It is something of a paradox that the linear programming model—with its finite number of processes, products, activities, and resource inputs—captures the multidimensional character of most real problems more easily and more quickly than do other methods and impresses upon one's mind the magnitude of the task of searching for an optimal course of action in a given complex real situation.

Another paradox is that while in some ways there is a roughness in the linear or piecewise linear approximations to reality, such approximations in a total sense usually are less crude than in traditional procedures, where various difficulties are frequently encountered. For example, the handling of numerous resource inputs usually results in an aggregation of different resource inputs to an uncomfortable degree. Conversely, in linear programming, the relative ease in representing in the model numerous resource inputs, some with definite limits on capacity or availability, permits much of the character of the real situation to be captured in a model. These limits may be imposed, for example, by a desire to attain particular levels of product or service quality or by environmental and population policies. The ability of a linear programming model to handle such maximum or minimum limits existing in the real world is a major advantage.

Finally, Harvard University, the University of Michigan, and the University of Nebraska have contributed greatly toward this effort.

Part I

Basic Economics and Decisions

1

Good Economic Thinking: Its Focus and Its Limitations

The aim of our study is to understand better the economic part of our lives in order to manage such affairs wisely. And we find the economic strand to be closely intertwined with other strands, making the task a challenging one.

Through it all, the economic aspect involves the common phenomenon of scarcity. Loosely speaking, this means that more of things are desired or needed than is available. Many goods and services, such as those involved in providing security, justice, and national defense, are "consumed" in a collective fashion. However, in these cases, as well as in others, scarcity is still involved.

Also, an understanding of the costs of things, which in a sense are indicators of relative scarcity in relation to their demand, requires viewing all buyers of a product or service to be taken together as well as all of the sellers.

Thus, our attention will focus at times on an individual person's or an individual firm's decision. At other times we shall look at all such decisions involving a specific product or service in the aggregate because of their effect on prices and the availabilities of goods and services.

The scarcity of goods and services to satisfy the desires of people implies the need for choices to be made. Thus, economic study focuses on decision making by individuals, organizations, and governments in making choices on the use of their limited resources such as time, money, land, equipment, facilities, or other such limited resources.

Much attention must be focused on the sources of goods and services (the entrepreneurs, managers, producers, etc.) who must make choices on what to produce with their limited resources and how it is to be produced (that is, the "techniques" to be used in production).

Furthermore, people in a free society viewed in the aggregate "decide" (without full awareness) through a system of markets or political institutions on *what* goods and services are produced by the whole system, *how* and *where* they are produced, and more or less, *how much* each person receives of society's total output.

We surely agree that the complex economic reality that we seek to understand presents a challenge. We want to become familiar with the best thinking available to us from the past as well as new ways of viewing and thinking about economic questions. Thus, our job is that of trying to understand well how our complex economic and business world functions and then, also, trying to learn how to make good assessments of what might happen in real situations and to make good decisions in those situations both in our work and our private lives.

We will try to take a more "hands-on" approach so the discussion does not seem so remote from reality. We will focus on *decisions* by consumers, firms, and government. Hence, we will use the simple "possibilities" tables and graphs where appropriate and illustrate the principles of rational decision making using "decision trees."

Good assessments of real situations (that is, assessing well what might happen and what is the best thing to do) require, first of all, an awareness that real situations are usually too rich, too diverse, and too interrelated and ever-changing for us to be able to capture them fully in our thinking. And this is true whether the thinking is formal or whether it is informal and intuitive.

Thus, invariably we have to leave much of reality out of our thinking, which of course makes the thinking somewhat incomplete. This commonly results in errors in the prediction of events and subsequent errors in decision making. We need to remember that real events may be caused, in part, at least, by factors we did not take into account. (Note: If, as the great philosophers have asserted, in a deep sense all reality is interrelated and past reality creates future reality, to attain perfect prediction and perfect decision we would have to incorporate all of reality and its interrelatedness into our thinking, which, of course, is impossible.)

The overriding need, then, is to try to identify, in light of our current knowledge, those elements in reality that are most important on which to focus so as to predict well and to make good decisions.

2

Free Markets: A Subtle and Decentralized System of Decision and Control Over Resource Use

The study of economics exists because of the limitations in the availability of resources needed to produce the goods and services we want. Simply put, the land, labor, equipment, and facilities used to produce one product are not at the same time available to produce other products. Therefore, choices have to be made on the uses of the available resources. These choices involve at least four interrelated decisions. They are:

1. *What* goods and services are to be produced with the limited resources (and how much of each).
2. *For Whom* the goods and service are to be produced; that is, "who is to get them."
3. *How* the goods and services are to be produced; that is, "by what technology."
4. *Where* they are to be produced; that is, the location of the production.

The need for making these decisions appears in some way in all economic systems, both those small and simple, and those large and complex. At one extreme we see the need arising in the isolated self-sufficient frontier farm family; at the other, we see the need in the modern, complex, and interdependent economy involving millions of individuals. In the latter, however, there exists extreme specialization of labor, equipment, and facilities along with the necessary use of money and markets for the pricing and allocation decisions involving the many products, services, and resources. Also, the goods and services consumed are for the most part goods and services created by others.

In the case of the frontier farm, the family can simply make all of the four decisions more or less directly without involving outside entities. Essentially, family members see that "what they produce is what they get." In the modern economy, however, these decisions, subtle and often spontaneous, involve many people, firms, markets, and governments. But here, too, we find that the amount of goods and services available to the people depends on how much is produced in the entire system.

Because of the dominant role played by free markets in making these four decisions, we need to examine in more detail just how free markets perform these functions of arriving at the decisions and also in controlling the use of resources.

What Goods and Services Are to Be Produced and in What Quantities

In a modern real economy, many different products and services can be produced with the resources available. We say that the resources limit the "possibilities" for the production of goods and services.

To help convey the nature of these limitations and to make them a bit more concrete we can construct a simple numerical *production-possibilities graph*, as shown in Figure 2.1. Of course, this is only a "concept" graph indicating the general nature of the basic economic problem.

The shaded region in Figure 2.1 represents possibilities for the production of the two products. We can think of Product 1 as being "consumer goods" such as clothing and Product 2 as "capital goods" such as machines. The *resource limitation line* marks the boundary of all of the possible output combinations of Product 1 and Product 2.

Table 2.1 shows a basic data table that lies behind the graph in Figure 2.1. From this table we constructed the graph in Figure 2.1. Thus, given the resource amount of 12 hours for a period (in reality, more like hundreds of thousands of hours of labor or machines) Product 1 with its rate of use of 2 hours would permit 6 units of Product 1 to be made if all resources were devoted to it. Product 2 would then have an output of 0.

Figure 2.1   **A Production-Possibilities Graph**

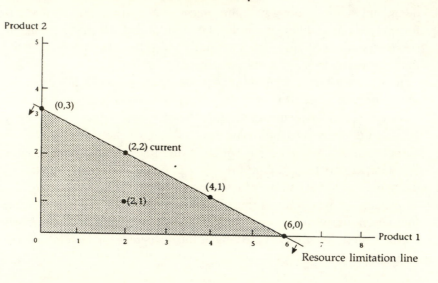

Analogously, the point (0,3) represents the output combination if all resources were devoted to making Product 2. Other points on a straight line drawn between the two points above represent possible combinations of the two products in light of the resource availability of 12 hours. A possible combination that does not lie on the limitation line is the point (2,1). Such points are associated with the failure to use all resources fully. If such a combination were to occur it would likely be temporary.

At times, we may construct a table showing selected combinations of the outputs of the products that are possible, such as is done in Table 2.2. In effect, a choice can be made from these combinations or the numerous other combinations represented by points on the resource limitation line in Figure 2.1.

Table 2.1

Basic Data Table

	Rates of resource use (in hours)		Resources available
	Product 1	Product 2	
Resources	2	4	12

Table 2.2

Product Combinations Table: Selected Combinations of Product 1 and Product 2 That Are Possible

Product 1	Product 2
0	3
2	2
4	1
6	0

We have selected a (2,2) point in Figure 2.1 as a possible mix of the two products currently preferred. The point represents 2 units of output of each product. Then, let us suppose a change in relative preference occurs regarding the two products. A greater preference is indicated for Product 1 compared to Product 2. And in response to this change, suppose a shift occurs in production toward Product 1 and away from Product 2 to the (4,1) point in Figure 2.1.

Because the new mix is 4 of Product 1 and 1 of Product 2 we say that the "trade-off" is as follows: By giving up 1 unit of Product 2 we get 2 more units of Product 1. The limited resource availability clearly requires the sacrifice of Product 2 in order to get more of Product 1. In the more complex real economy, however, the trade-off rates may not remain constant as we have assumed here.

In a free market system this change in relative preference for the products would give rise to an "increase in demand" for Product 1 and a "decrease in demand" for Product 2. This starts a series of responses in the markets, as depicted in Figure 2.2.

As seen in Figure 2.2, the increase in demand for a product in a free market system is *not* transmitted to a central point in the system but only to local points of production (firms). The local points (the firms) respond by changing their production programs and by going to the resource markets for more of the necessary resource inputs to increase the output in response to the potential for greater profit by producing the product in greater demand.

For Whom the Goods and Services Are to Be Produced

Those receiving money income have access to the goods and services produced. In a free market system, money incomes are determined by the prices arrived at in the resource markets for resources actually pro-

Figure 2.2 **The Free Market System: A Depiction of the Subtle System for Decision and Control Over Resource Use in Producing Goods and Services for Which Greater Consumer Preference Is Indicated**

Current demand and supply situation for a product or a service → Increase in demand for a product → Increases the price of the product → Increases the immediate profit for each firm, and also more profit still if additional resource inputs can be hired quickly, like labor (a variable input) → Increases the firm's demand for the variable resource inputs (labor, raw materials, etc.) → Increases the variable resource prices (wages, etc.) which draw these resources from other uses in order to produce the product for which greater preference was shown vided in production, the prices going by the names of *wages* and *salaries*, *fees*, *rents*, *interest*, *profits*, and *dividends*.

For a moment, suppose everyone in an economic system has the same money incomes and wealth along with free choice regarding their use. In this situation the output of goods and services in a given period would tend to go to people somewhat in accord with the strength of their preferences for the different products.

Consider the very scarce outputs that might be strongly preferred by some, perhaps many, people. The market price may be quite high—too high for some in light of their strength of preference for these products and services in relation to others. The scarce output would then tend to go to those whose preference for these products or services was exceptionally strong. They would be willing to deny themselves many other products in order to buy those that are exceptionally scarce and high in price and that absorb much of their money income or assets.

In a typical real market-driven economic system, money incomes and wealth are not equal, usually because money incomes are determined in resource input markets. The resource prices, so to speak, are the money wages, rents, interest, and profits that are based largely on the value of the contributions to the production of the goods and services.

Thus, with disparities in money incomes, allocation of the final goods and services on the basis of the relative strength of preferences is modified somewhat. Some individuals, with higher money incomes, can acquire scarce and higher-priced goods and services without much sacrifice of other goods and services. Thus, they may obtain these scarce items even though their preferences for them are not exceptionally strong.

But the differences in money incomes created in the production of goods and services play an important role in bringing forth large amounts of goods and services in the first place. Essentially, the main forces tend to work this way: Final products and services that are strongly preferred, but relatively scarce, usually will result in higher prices in the market. This, in turn, will cause the value of the contributions of resources to the production process to be high and give those supplying these scarce resources higher monetary returns (wages, rents, interest, and profits). And importantly, the higher monetary returns pull more resources into the production of the scarce products and services and in turn can lead to lower product prices. Thus, the higher return to such resources plays an important role in providing incentives to bring forth a higher level of production of those goods and services for which great preference is shown.

How the Goods and Services Are to Be Produced: The Technology

This decision involves the choice of techniques (or processes) used in producing a good or service. Some processes that are used to make a given product require much labor (as in hand processes), whereas other processes involve less labor (as in mechanized processes). And different processes incur different costs because each process usually uses different amounts of each resource in producing a unit of a product. In a free market system the competition between firms forces each of them to use the lowest-cost technique in order to maintain sufficient profit. It turns out that in some labor-surplus countries this could mean employing a process that uses labor heavily, whereas in other cases a low labor-using process wins out.

Where the Products Are to Be Produced

Some of the firms making a specific product may be located in different regions of the world, yet they compete with each other in selling their products to the buyers. Each location typically has different costs; this is especially so for raw materials, labor, and for transporting the product to buyers, who often are located at many different points throughout the world.

Analogous to the case of technology, a free market system with strong competition between firms forces production to take place where the total costs of production per unit of output are at a minimum. Naturally, in some current international markets, tariffs, subsidies, and quotas can alter the actual location of production.

Still another decision lies in the background. This decision involves the choice of how much of current resources to use for current consumption goods and services and how much to use for goods and services (such as machines and facilities) that would *increase production possibilities in the future*.

If all resources are currently being used, this decision involves a sacrifice of consumption goods and services in order to produce capital goods (such as machines and facilities), research services, and educational services, all of which can increase future production possibilities.

Investment in capital goods, for example, increases the *resources* that will be available for greater production of goods and services in the

Table 2.3

Basic Data Table After Increase in Productivity Leading to a 25 Percent Decrease in Rates of Resource Use (in hours)

	Product 1	Product 2	Resources available
Resources	1.5	3	12

future. Also, devoting more of the current resources to education and research can increase the *productivity* of resources, such as labor.

A simple numerical example of the latter factor is shown in Table 2.3. Here, the original production possibilities shown in Table 2.1 have been altered to illustrate the effect on production possibilities of a 25 percent *decrease* in the rate of use of the resources by each product (because of the increased productivity). Product 2, for example, now requires only 3 hours instead of 4 hours. The new production-possibilities graph is shown in Figure 2.3. The resource limitation line now has shifted outward and permits an expanded region of production possibilities. More of each product can now be produced, and, if desired, more of both products.

The free market system relies on firms and individuals to foresee the greater return, such as profit, from investing in capital goods, resources, and education. Of course, in actual systems, governments have, especially in the case of education and research, supplemented private outlays because of the limited foresight or motivation on the part of firms and individuals.

Figure 2.3 **New Production Possibilities Due to Increased Productivity**

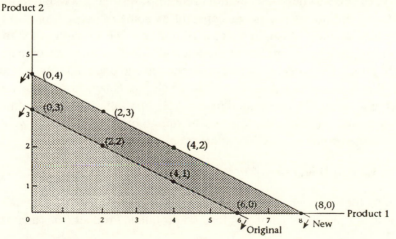

3

Consumer Decision, Product Demand, and Market Price

In a smoothly functioning free market system, consumer decisions tend to determine the allocation of resources to the production of various products and services. A separate market, more or less, exists for each final product, consumers constituting the "demand" side of the market and producers (firms) the "supply" side.

In each of these markets we observe two common relationships. One of these patterns is called the "law of demand," the other the "law of supply." In most all markets we observe that buyers of a product or service will tend to purchase more of it at lower prices. This is called the "law of demand." In the case of producers the common pattern is for more of the product to be produced at higher prices. This is called the "law of supply."

These "laws" describe common relationships that are found in markets but are not as precise or constant as some of those found in the physical sciences. Also, in the case of markets, the strength of the relationship varies from market to market and also over time. In some markets, buyers (and sellers, too) are quite sensitive to price changes, whereas in other markets little sensitivity to price changes may exist. Thus, much of the challenge in understanding markets in a future period lies in understanding the future response of buyers to different prices as well as the future response of sellers to different possible prices.

The Law of Demand in More Detail

Let us look at a simple example that illustrates the law of demand. A consumer has a budget of $24 for two products. Product 1 has a current

Table 3.1

Consumption-Possibilities Table: Budget of $24 for Two Products

	Price per unit		Resource amount
	Product 1	Product 2	available: budget
Resource: Budget	$8	$4	$24
	(Varied to $6, then $3)		

price of $8 and Product 2 a price of $4. We record this data in Table 3.1.

When plotted, the data in Table 3.1 give us a *budget limitation line,* as shown in Figure 3.1(a). If the entire $24 budget is spent on Product 1 (with its $8 price), we see that 3 units can be obtained. Spending it all on Product 2 (with its $4 price) yields 6 units. A line drawn through these two points [that is, the (3,0) point and the (0,6) point] creates the relevant $24 budget limitation line at the current prices.

Various possible combinations of Product 1 and Product 2 lie on the budget limitation line, and we assume our consumer chooses the (1,4) combination—that is, 1 unit of Product 1 and 4 units of Product 2. The law of demand, however, involves possible changes in the price of a product and the response of buyers to the changes. Let us focus on our consumer's demand for Product 1.

Suppose the price of Product 1 drops to $6 from its current $8. First, this means a new budget limitation line exists, as shown in Figure 3.1(b), and new combinations of the two products are possible.

Figure 3.1   **Consumer Decision Responding to Price Changes**

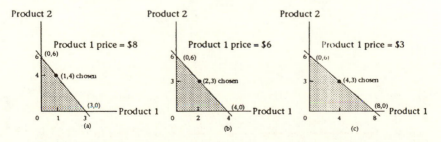

Consumer's assumed decision as Product 1 price alone varies from $8 to $6, then to $3. The budget remains at $24. Product 2 price stays the same at $4.

Table 3.2

Consumer's Demand Schedule When the Budget Is $24. An Illustration of the Law of Demand: The Quantity Demanded for a Product Increases as Its Price Decreases

Price of product 1	Quantity demanded of product 1
$8	1 unit
$6	2 units
$3	4 units

Suppose further that our consumer now chooses the (2,3) combination, which means 2 units of Product 1 (one more than before) in response to the Product 1 price decrease. At the price of $8, 1 unit was chosen, whereas now under the $6 price, 2 units are chosen. This reveals a portion of this consumer's *demand schedule*, as recorded in Table 3.2.

In Table 3.2 we also record the assumed response due to the Product 1 price falling to $3. The new budget line, and the (4,3) combination chosen, appear in Figure 3.1(c). Four units of Product 1 are now chosen under this Product 1 price.

The demand schedule data in Table 3.2 when graphed give us the downsloping demand curve *d* shown in Figure 3.2. While it is usual for only one price to exist in a pure market, a demand curve shows the

Figure 3.2   **A Consumer Demand Curve**

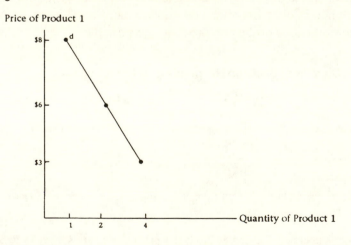

The individual consumer's Product 1 demand curve when the budget is $24.

Figure 3.3 **A Market Demand Curve With a Market Supply Curve**

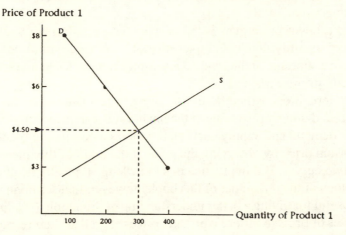

The entire demand curve *D* for Product 1 by 100 identical consumers along with a typical upsloping supply curve representing the firms' responses to different possible Product 1 prices. The market price for Product 1 would settle at $4.50 where the curves intersect.

quantity of the product assumed to be demanded *at various possible prices*, were they to exist.

Free markets typically are comprised of many buyers and many sellers. The demand for a product by all buyers taken together gives the basis for a demand curve for the entire market. We call such a curve a *market demand curve* and label it *D*.

If the demand side of our market is comprised of (say) 100 identical consumers, such as the one in Figure 3.2, we have a market demand curve D for Product 1, as shown in Figure 3.3. Also shown is a typical upsloping supply curve *S* representing the response of sellers supplying greater quantities at higher prices.

Rather dramatically, we see that the market price for Product 1 would settle at $4.50 where the two curves intersect (Figure 3.3). We call this price the "equilibrium" price because the quantity demanded by the buyers would equal the quantity supplied by the sellers. This means that all of Product 1 placed on the market at that price would be taken by the buyers. The units supplied would be 300 and the units demanded would also be 300. There would be no surplus of Product 1, and no buyers would go unsatisfied.

If a higher price were to exist temporarily (say at $6.00), it would not last because an excess of the quantity supplied over the quantity demanded at that price would result in the market price falling to the market-clearing price of $4.50.

Were a lower price than $4.50 to exist temporarily (say $4.00), an excess of quantity demanded over quantity supplied would occur, resulting in a shortage of the product and a subsequent rise in market price to the equilibrium price of $4.50.

Therefore, if one would be able to know, in real situations, the future demand-and-supply responses of the buyers and sellers in a market (that is, their demand and supply curves), it would be possible to predict the equilibrium price by observing the price at the point of the intersection of the two curves. But in practice this knowledge typically is quite elusive. Much of the remainder of this book, however, focuses upon procedures useful for giving a better understanding of the supply (production) responses of firms to different product prices as well as their response to other factors.

Shifts in Demand and Supply Affect Market-Clearing Prices

Buyers' decisions (and sellers' decisions, too) are indeed influenced by prices they confront for a product, but their decisions also may be influenced by factors *other than the price of the product.*

When these "other" factors influence the decisions of buyers or sellers, a "shift" in demand or supply will occur. Thus, the demand curve or the supply curve will shift its position, affecting the intersection point and thus the market-clearing price.

For example, a change in the budgets (or incomes) of consumers often affects their purchase decisions. And this development, in turn, tends to affect the equilibrium price of the product. Let us illustrate this:

An increase in a consumer's budget (say from $24 to $36, as shown in Table 3.3) may increase the amount purchased at an existing price. Suppose the price existing is $8 (as in our original example) and 1 unit is purchased. Now, after the consumer's budget rises from $24 to $36, the purchase of 2 units would be desired at the same $8 price. Usually, at various prices that might exist, more would be purchased after the budget increases. Responses in our example are recorded in Table 3.4. In Figure 3.4 we graph the new demand data along with the original demand data in Figure 3.2. We label the new demand curve d^1 and see that it represents a shift from the original demand curve d.

Table 3.3

The Consumer's New Data Table: The Budget Increases to $36 for the Two Products

| | Price per unit | | |
	Product 1	Product 2	Resource amount available: budget
Resource: Budget	$8 (varied to $6, then $3)	$4	$36 (new)

Table 3.4

Consumer's New Demand Schedule When the Budget Is $36.
An Illustration of a Shift in Demand: The Quantity Demanded of a Product Changes Due to Factors Other Than Its Price, Such as an Increase in a Consumer's Budget

Price of product 1	Quantity demanded of product 1
$8	2 units
$6	4 units
$3	8 units

In Figure 3.4 we see an upward shift in the demand for the product by our single consumer due to the budget increase.

Looking toward the entire market and simplifying again, suppose we have 100 such identical consumers. We now graph the new aggregate demand curve D^1 on top of those in Figure 3.3, and obtain the graphs in Figure 3.5.

With the shift in demand from demand curve D to demand curve D^1 we see a new point of intersection with the original upsloping supply curve.

The new equilibrium price in the market will be $5.75. The upward shift in demand has increased the market-clearing price from $4.50 to $5.75.

Now at the higher product price we see something else of importance. Producers are now induced to place more on the market *at the higher market price* and would draw resources to its production.

Say there are 100 identical firms each producing 3 units at the original equilibrium price of $4.50, resulting in a total quantity supplied of 300 units. But when the market price rises, firms commonly find it prof-

Figure 3.4 A Shift in Consumer's Demand Curve

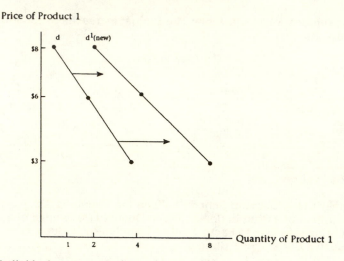

The individual consumer's demand curve shifts to the right when the budget increases from $24 to $36.

Figure 3.5 A Shift in the Market Demand Curve

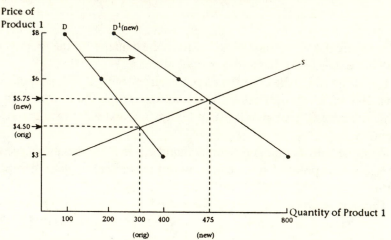

A shift in the entire demand curve for Product 1 occurs as all 100 consumers respond in the same way to increases in their budgets. The original market-clearing price of $4.50 gives way to the higher $5.75.

itable to hire more resources and to produce more units. Here, we have assumed that at the price of $5.75 it is most profitable for each firm to produce 4¾ units, giving rise to a total amount supplied of 475 from all

Figure 3.6 **The Free Market System: Graphic Depiction of the Subtle System for Decision and Control Over Resource Use in Producing Goods and Services for Which Greater Consumer Preference Is Indicated**

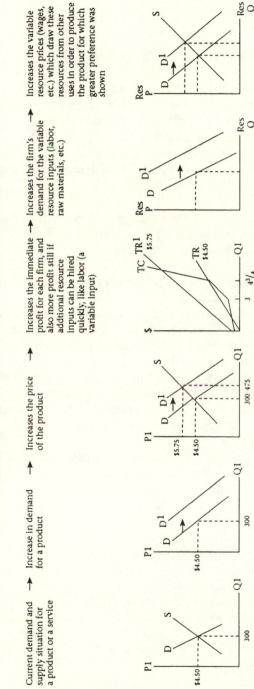

Box 3.1

Public Policy Intervention in Markets

Although free markets tend to induce firms and resource owners to respond to consumer preferences revealed in the product markets, for various reasons their actual operations often need intervention by some level of government to serve social objectives.

The following is a partial listing of some of the more prominent interventions that different levels of government might take, some of which will be discussed in later chapters.

- Various actions that attempt to improve the information available to firms and consumers regarding prices, production, and employment.
- Various policies that attempt to maintain effective competition in markets where it is feasible through antimonopoly laws and related policies against collusion by firms, including deception and noncompetitive practices.
- Price controls (including wage controls) during extremely disruptive periods such as those occurring during wartime.
- Minimum wage controls as an attempt to increase the income of a segment of the labor force.
- Subsidies to firms and individuals as an attempt to induce higher productivity and more rational action through education, or to attain greater benefit for some segment of the population because of temporary immobility or other impediments to an effective response to market forces.
- Supporting agriculture prices at higher than equilibrium levels in order to provide temporary aid to agricultural producers. This has been a frustrating approach, however, generating sizable surpluses with accompanying disposal problems. Consequently, aid has more recently taken the form of cooperative output restrictions to attain desired price levels as well as the use of direct subsidies.
- Taxation and expenditure policies to finance security and infrastructure (such as highways) that affect after-tax incomes of individuals and firms.
- Controls over the safety and quality of specific products and services such as food, health, medicine, transportation, and fuels.

100 firms. And this price would tend to last as all 475 units would be purchased at $5.75. We try to capture this sequence in Figure 3.6. The underlying basis for the firms' decisions on optimal profit output will be explored in subsequent chapters.

In this chapter we have illustrated a "shift" in demand due to an income or budget change for the consumers. Increases or decreases in consumer preferences for a product would have similar shifting effects on demand. And, as we shall see in some detail in later chapters, technological changes and other factors can shift the supply curves of firms from their current position. Thus, equilibrium prices change as both supply curves and demand curves shift.

Elasticity of Demand

"Elasticity of demand" for a product is a measure of the price sensitivity of buyers of the product over some price range. A quantitative measure, called the "coefficient of elasticity," is obtained by computing the ratio of the percent change in quantity demanded to a given percent change in the product price.

"Unit elasticity," which denotes a coefficient of 1.00, occurs when the percent changes in price and quantity demanded are the same in absolute value (one increasing and the other decreasing).

Coefficients greater than 1.00 denote an "elastic" demand when, over some range, the percent decrease in quantity demanded is greater than a given percent increase in price.

Coefficients less than 1.00 reveal an "inelastic" demand (common for products viewed as necessities) where the percent decrease in quantity demanded is less than the percent increase in price. Loosely speaking, such products are associated with a steep, downsloping demand curve. At the extreme, a product with a "perfectly inelastic" demand would have no decrease in quantity demanded at all when the product price increases, resulting in a vertical demand curve and an elasticity coefficient of .00.

4

Underlying Physical Aspects of Production Decisions

To gain a better understanding of the supply side of markets we need to examine in some detail the basis for the production decisions by firms in various circumstances.

This requires that we get "inside" individual firms, so to speak, and view the decision making from their standpoint. Then, aggregating the product output decisions of all the firms in an industry gives us the basis for developing a supply curve for the entire product market.

We shall assume that each firm seeks the level of output of a product or service that maximizes its total profit after all costs have been taken into account.

Thus, it becomes necessary to incorporate into our analysis such things as the cost of all resource inputs (such as labor, equipment, etc.), the various technological processes available along with their rates of use of each of the resources, and the price that can be obtained for the final product.

We shall call the output where total profit is greatest the *optimal output*. As we shall see, in some contexts this may not be the maximum output possible. By hiring more resources, output might be higher but the additional costs incurred may exceed the additional revenue, creating, in turn, a drop in total profit.

The usual underlying cause of this is the well-known "law of diminishing returns." Another factor can arise from the relationship, known as "returns to scale." Both factors involve physical relationships and are crucial to a good understanding of the economic forces involving the firm. We shall now focus on these forces and illustrate them with a simple numerical model of a firm. In Diagram 4.1, using a numerical illustration, we assemble the necessary underlying physical data of a firm. Every firm has a physical basis, and thus it is necessary to understand it to determine the optimal profit output of a product or service.

Our simple example assumes that a single product is to be made (say, jackets) and only two resource inputs are necessary. These resources are sewing machine hours and labor hours. The labor is needed to operate the machines or for hand sewing. In real situations more resource inputs than two would be typical, but they could simply be added to those we have already specified.

Let us refer to the machine hours as Resource 1 (R_1) and labor hours as Resource 2 (R_2). Currently, we have specific amounts of each resource available, which are fixed for a limited time. We have Resource 1 fixed at 6 hours and Resource 2 fixed at 2 hours. Of course, in practical situations, the inputs would likely be in the hundreds of hours, but our purpose here is to illustrate as simply as possible the important physical aspects bearing on the firm as it considers its production decision, which ultimately takes costs and revenues into account as well.

Now to the technological aspects. Our firm uses two different techniques, or "processes," to make the product. Process 1 is more of a hand process using labor heavily, whereas Process 2 is more mechanized. Figure 4.1 offers a conceptual depiction.

The small data table at the left in Diagram 4.1 captures what we need to begin our analysis. The current resource amounts (Res Amt) available are shown in the right-hand column of the data table. The two other columns in the table record the *rates of use* of Resource 1 and Resource 2 *per unit of product output* by each process.

Thus, reading the data table vertically, Process 1 (the hand process, P_1) uses 2 hours of machine time and 2 hours of labor for each unit of product by that process. Analogously, Process 2 (the mechanized process, P_2) uses 3 hours of machine time and only 1 hour of labor for each unit produced. We can think of the different processes as different "recipes" for making the product.

A graphic representation of the information in the data table is shown below the table in Diagram 4.1. On the horizontal axis we represent product output by Process 1 and on the vertical axis output by Process 2. (Later we use X_1 to represent possible output by Process 1 and X_2 to represent output by Process 2.)

Diagram 4.1 **Maximization of Output in the Firm Over Different Time Periods With Two Resources and Two Processes Available**

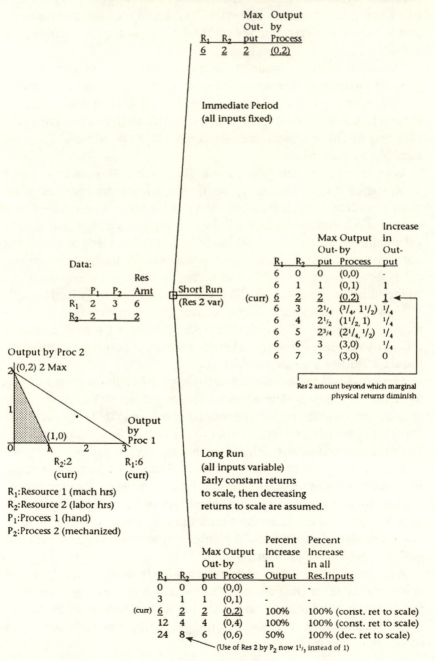

R₁	R₂	Max Out-put	Output by Process
6	2	2	(0,2)

Immediate Period
(all inputs fixed)

Data:

	P₁	P₂	Res Amt
R₁	2	3	6
R₂	2	1	2

Short Run
(Res 2 var)

	R₁	R₂	Max Out-put	Output by Process	Increase in Out-put
	6	0	0	(0,0)	-
	6	1	1	(0,1)	1
(curr)	6	2	2	(0,2)	1
	6	3	2¼	(³/₄, 1½)	¼
	6	4	2½	(1½, 1)	¼
	6	5	2¾	(2¼, ½)	¼
	6	6	3	(3,0)	¼
	6	7	3	(3,0)	0

Res 2 amount beyond which marginal physical returns diminish

Output by Proc 2

2 (0,2) 2 Max

1

(1,0)

O   1   2   3

R₂:2   R₁:6
(curr)   (curr)

Output by Proc 1

R₁:Resource 1 (mach hrs)
R₂:Resource 2 (labor hrs)
P₁:Process 1 (hand)
P₂:Process 2 (mechanized)

Long Run
(all inputs variable)
Early constant returns
to scale, then decreasing
returns to scale are assumed.

	R₁	R₂	Max Out-put	Output by Process	Percent Increase in Output	Percent Increase in all Res.Inputs
	0	0	0	(0,0)	-	-
	3	1	1	(0,1)	-	-
(curr)	6	2	2	(0,2)	100%	100% (const. ret to scale)
	12	4	4	(0,4)	100%	100% (const. ret to scale)
	24	8	6	(0,6)	50%	100% (dec. ret to scale)

(Use of Res 2 by P₂ now 1¹/₃ instead of 1)

Figure 4.1 **Conceptual Depiction of the Creation of Product Output by Different Processes From a Set of Resource Inputs**

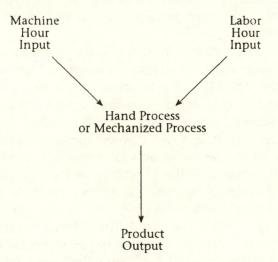

Machine
Hour
Input

Labor
Hour
Input

Hand Process
or Mechanized Process

Product
Output

Each resource *row* in the data table gives us in the graph a "limitation line" imposed by that resource. Taking each row separately, we see from the data table that by using Process 1 alone, Resource 1 would impose a limit of 3 units of output: 6/2 = 3. By Process 2 alone, Resource 1 would limit us to only 2 units of output: 6/3 = 2. Assuming the rates of usage hold fast, we can connect the two points on the axes with a straight line to obtain the current Resource 1 limitation line.

Of course, Resource 2 also imposes limitations. Looking at Resource 2 separately, we see that by Process 1 alone only 1 unit of output would be possible: 2/2 = 1. By Process 2 it could be 2 units of output: 2/1 = 2. Connecting the two points on the axes gives us the current Resource 2 limitation line.

Because we must consider only programs of production by the processes that are possible in light of both resource limitations, we are restricted to the shaded area in the graph in Diagram 4.1.

It is clear from the graph that the total output is maximized by producing 2 units by Process 2 and none by Process 1; that is, the (0,2) program (thus, $X_1 = 0$ and $X_2 = 2$).

The rest of Diagram 4.1 involves a tree diagram that flows conceptually from left to right.

We begin with the "decision point" enclosed by the small square in the center of Diagram 4.1. Three branches emanate from the decision point, each representing a different future time period. Focusing on each of the time periods essentially constitutes a separate course of action or "act."

Thus, a decision may be made for (1) the "Immediate Period" (top right of Diagram 4.1) when all resource inputs are fixed at their current levels; (2) the "Short Run" (middle right) where at least one but not all resource inputs may be varied in amount; or (3) the "Long Run" (bottom right) where all inputs may be varied in amount.

Our earlier discussion focused on the immediate period where all inputs were fixed. The maximum total output was found to be 2 units using the (0,2) program—that is, nothing by Process 1 and 2 units by Process 2. As seen in Diagram 4.1, this is recorded at the tip of the immediate-period branch at the top of the diagram.

The second branch in Diagram 4.1 (middle right) represents the act of focusing on the short run where we assume one of the resources can be varied. It is Resource 2 (labor hours). Resource 1 (machine hours) remains fixed at 6 hours.

At the tip of this branch we record eight different resource input combinations and the maximum output consequence of each combination. For this simple example, the maximum output program for each combination of the inputs can be obtained graphically, as in Figure 4.2. The current Resource 2 input amount in Figure 4.2 is identified at 2, and the Resource 2 limit line is shifted outward as it is increased in amount, giving larger and larger shaded feasible regions with a new maximum output program at a corner point of each new shaded area.

The last column in the short-run analysis table of Diagram 4.1, "Increase in Output," gives us a clear-cut illustration of the famous "law of diminishing marginal physical returns." In its most basic form, this "law" is usually defined as follows: As a variable input is added to a fixed input (or inputs) the increase in total output from each *additional* unit of the variable input will *eventually* decline.

In our example, the increase in output from each additional unit of the variable Resource 2 input remains constant at 1 unit of output for the first and second units of Resource 2. However, the increase in output falls to ¼ unit of output as the third unit of Resource 2 is added. The Resource 2 input of 2 thus indicates the point beyond which diminishing marginal physical returns begin in the example.

Figure 4.2 **Maximum Output Programs When Resource 2 Varies From Zero to 6**

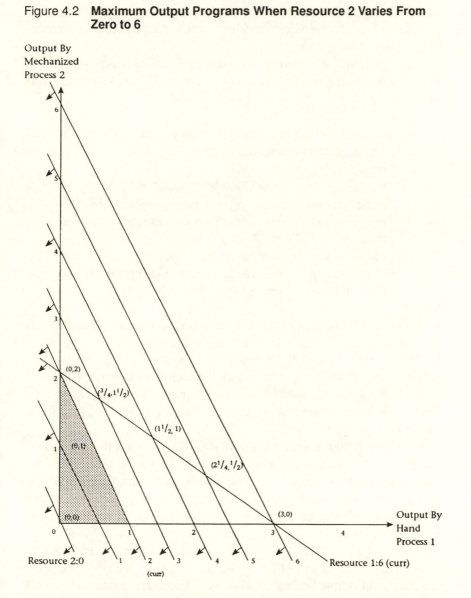

Output By
Mechanized
Process 2

The "marginal physical product," as the increase in output is often called, stays at ¼ unit through the sixth Resource 2 input. The seventh unit of Resource 2 input results in no increase at all in total output, so it is said to have a marginal physical product of zero.

The third branch (bottom) in Diagram 4.1 represents a third alternative: focusing on the "long run" when all resource inputs may be varied. The main ideas involved here are illustrated by the possible occurrences of one of the following events.

If all inputs are increased by the same percent (such as 100 percent), one of the following results will occur as the "scale" of the operations is increased:

(a) *Constant returns to scale* where output also increases by 100 percent (the *same* percent increase as the percent increase in *all* inputs).

(b) *Decreasing returns to scale* where output increases by *less* than the 100 percent increase in the inputs (output may increase but the *percent increase in output is lower than the percent increase in all inputs*).

(c) *Increasing returns to scale* where output increases by *more* than the 100 percent increase in all inputs (a *higher* percent increase in output than the percent increase in all inputs).

In our simple example with only two resource inputs, we illustrate the possibilities of "returns to scale" by increasing both resource inputs by 100 percent increments. Results of doing this in our example are shown at the tip of the third branch at the bottom of Diagram 4.1.

Start with Resource 1 and Resource 2 inputs at 3 and 1, respectively. With those inputs we see that maximum total output is 1 unit, obtainable by the (0,1) program.

Increasing both resource inputs by 100 percent raises the Resource 1 and Resource 2 inputs to 6 and 2, respectively. And if the rates of resource use by the processes hold fast at the original rates, the maximum output would be 2 units obtained by the (0,2) program. Thus, output increases by 100 percent (1 unit to 2 units) as *all inputs* increase by 100 percent. In this range we have "constant returns to scale." If both Resource 1 and 2 inputs are increased by another 100 percent to 12 and 4, respectively, maximum output would be 4 units by the (0,4) program. Because total output increased also by 100 percent again, we have a continuation of the range where "constant returns to scale" exist.

But it looks like trouble for our firm as it increases Resource 1 and 2 inputs by another 100 percent to 24 and 8, respectively. This is seen to yield 6 units of output with the (0,6) program, which is only a 50 percent increase over the 4 units prior to the 100 percent input increases. This indicates a region of "decreasing returns to scale," and, as we shall see in later discussions, is crucial in increasing the costs per unit of output as the scale of operations increases.

Looking more closely at our illustration, we see in Diagram 4.1 (at the tip of the lower long-run branch) that if the recent increase in scale were to occur, an increase in the underlying rate of use of Resource 2 (labor hours) by Process 2 is assumed to rise to $1^{1}/_{3}$ hours from only 1 hour. This means that, at that scale of operations, the productivity of Resource 2 would fall from 1 unit of output per hour to ¾ unit per hour. Productivity rates are usually defined as rates of output per unit of input, whereas our "rates of use" values refer to the rate of use of an input per unit of output. Thus, the productivity rate of a resource, such as Resource 2 in this range, is the reciprocal of the rate of use of that resource; the reciprocal of $1^{1}/_{3}$ is $^{3}/_{4.}$ Another illustration comes from gasoline consumption in driving my car. If I get 20 miles per gallon (i.e., its productivity per gallon of input), I can also say that it uses $^{1}/_{20}$ of a gallon per mile (i.e., its rate of use of gasoline per mile of output).

"Increasing returns to scale" can occur over some range in some industries where specialization and division of labor can lead to increased productivity of resources, thus decreasing rates of use per unit of output. In this case, the doubling of all inputs would more than double total output with subsequent decreases in costs per unit of output. This tends to encourage firms to become larger, but while it may be unclear in what range increasing returns to scale will occur or continue to occur, all firms seem to be faced ultimately with decreasing returns to scale and a limit to their size. Management skill, however, seems to play a big role in affecting the point at which decreasing returns to scale begin for a specific firm.

Bases of Effective Influence Over Operations Within Firms That Affect the Returns to Scale

Aside from the pure technological aspects of operations that affect the returns to scale in a specific firm, there are a number of essentially nontechnological factors that can significantly influence whether, as the firm increases its scale, increasing returns can be realized with the consequence of decreasing average total costs.

The following are some of the main bases of influence aside from the technological basis:

- *Information:* The flow of accurate, relevant knowledge, including efficient accounting and information systems.
- *Incentives:* An effective broad-based incentive system that encourages creativity, efficiency, and the realization of the assumed rates of resource use (i.e., resource productivities).
- *Legitimacy:* The existence of clear standards of performance in a context of widely held expectations of wholehearted acceptance and compliance of proposed actions.
- *Status:* The effective use of hierarchical status within the firm to realize efficient performance. Also, the effective use of functional status within some area of knowledge to achieve efficient performance.

Problems

4.1   An item of furniture is made by a firm that considers two processes by which it can be made. The following data table shows the current availabilities of two resources (machine hours and labor hours) and their rates of usage by the two processes.

	Process 1	Process 2	Resource amount available
Resource 1 (machine hours)	2 hours	4 hours	8 hours
Resource 2 (labor hours)	3 hours	1 hour	2 hours

   (a) Which process is more labor-intensive?
   (b) For the immediate period, determine graphically the current maximum output program revealing the maximum total output and the optimal output by each process when output is maximized.
   (c) By graphical methods, vary Resource 2 (labor hours) from 0 to 13 hours, it being fixed at 2 hours in the immediate period but may be changed in a future period. From the analysis, construct a table that shows for all whole number Resource 2 amounts the maximum output program (the output by each process), the maximum total output, and the increase in total output due to each additional unit input of Resource 2.
   (d) For Resource 2, what is the amount beyond which diminishing marginal physical returns begin?

4.2   Consider a firm that makes parts for automobile manufacturers. Its operations involving the production of one item are described in the following data table, which shows the availability of Resource 1 (machine hours) and Resource 2 (labor hours) for a period along with the rates of usage of each resource per unit of output by two processes.

	Process 1	Process 2	Resource amount available
Resource 1 (machine hours)	4 hours	2 hours	12 hours
Resource 2 (labor hours)	1 hour	2 hours	6 hours

(a) Which process is the more labor-intensive?

(b) Graphically determine for the immediate period the current maximum output program (the output by each process) and thus the maximum total output.

(c) Extend the graphical analysis in (b) by varying Resource 2 (labor hours) from 0 to 14 hours. Construct a table that shows for all whole number Resource 2 amounts the maximum output program, the maximum total output, and the increase in total output generated by each unit increment in Resource 2.

(d) For Resource 2, what is the point of diminishing marginal physical returns?

4.3   A firm makes shoes by two processes and has assembled the following data table indicating for a period the amounts available of Resource 1 (machine hours) and Resource 2 (labor hours) as well as their rates of usage per unit of output by each process:

	Process 1	Process 2	Resource amount available
Resource 1 (machine hours)	6 hours	4 hours	12 hours
Resource 2 (labor hours)	2 hours	4 hours	8 hours

(a) On graph paper, plot the two resource limitation lines and identify the current maximum output program (the output by each process) and thus the maximum total output for the immediate period.

(b) From the graph in (a), begin a short-run analysis by varying Resource 2 (labor hours) from 0 to 14. For all whole number Resource 2 amounts, record in a table the maximum output program, the maximum total output, and the increase in total output associated with each unit increment in Resource 2.

(c) Identify the Resource 2 amount beyond which diminishing marginal physical returns begin.

4.4 Backpacks are made by a firm that uses two processes and is limited by two resources available, namely machine hours and labor hours. The following data table gives the rates of usage of the resources per unit of output and the amount of each resource available for a given period:

	Process 1	Process 2	Resource amount available
Resource 1 (machine hours)	2 hours	3 hours	6 hours
Resource 2 (labor hours)	4 hours	2 hours	12 hours

(a) By the graphic method, obtain for the immediate period the current maximum output program and the maximum total output.
(b) Undertake an analysis of Resource 2 (labor hours) variation in the short run from 0 to 13 hours. Record in a table, for all whole number Resource 2 amounts, the maximum output program, the maximum total output, and the increase in total output associated with each unit increment in Resource 2.
(c) Identify the point of diminishing marginal physical returns for Resource 2 (that is, the point beyond which marginal physical returns are less).

4.5 Consider another firm in the industry of which our example firm in this chapter is a member. In this other firm's long-run planning it anticipates the following data on its returns to scale in light of some innovations it expects to make on the rates of use of the resources by Process 2. Verify graphically each of the maximum output programs for the selected resource input combinations.

Amount of Res 1	Amount of Res 2	Process 1 Rate of use of Res 1	Process 1 Rate of use of Res 2	Process 2 Rate of use of Res 1	Process 2 Rate of use of Res 2	Maximum output program	Maximum total output
0	0	2	2	3	1	(0,0)	0
3	1	2	2	3	1	(0,1)	1
6	2	2	2	3	1	(0,2)	2
12	4	2	2	3	$2/3$	(0,6)	6
24	8	2	2	$3 3/7$	1	(0,7)	7

Identify the ranges of resource amounts in the above table over which the following would exist:

(a) Constant returns to scale.
(b) Increasing returns to scale.
(c) Decreasing returns to scale.

5

Decision in the Firm: The Input Approach

Consideration of the physical aspects of production discussed in the previous chapter is crucial in decision making in the firm. However, in that chapter we did not incorporate either the costs of the resource inputs or the revenue from the output. For optimal decision making, all of these aspects need to be incorporated into the analysis as well. Both the output program and the set of resource inputs that maximize total profit are the assumed objectives, and in a free market system the firm must give these objectives high priority.

We shall see as we proceed through this chapter, as well as in those beyond, that when the firm seeks the output and resource input levels that maximize total profit, the maximization of output *and* the minimization of cost objectives in an implicit way are also served at different levels of each input and output.

In Diagram 5.1 we assemble the necessary data for our example to illustrate the optimal profit decision for each of the three time periods: the immediate period (when all resource inputs are fixed), the short run (when some but not all inputs can be varied), and the long run (when all inputs may be varied).

Diagram 5.1 takes the physical aspects from Diagram 4.1 in the previous chapter and incorporates the cost of the resources and the revenue from the output. Therefore, we have the essential data for determining the optimal profit decision.

The data table (middle left) in Diagram 5.1 includes the prices (and thus the cost) of the two resources: $3 for each unit of Resource 1 and $10 for each unit of Resource 2. The Resource 1 amount is fixed at 6, indicating that we are leasing machines at $3 per hour and have committed ourselves to 6 hours.

Diagram 5.1 Cost, Revenue, and Profit Analysis Using the Input Approach

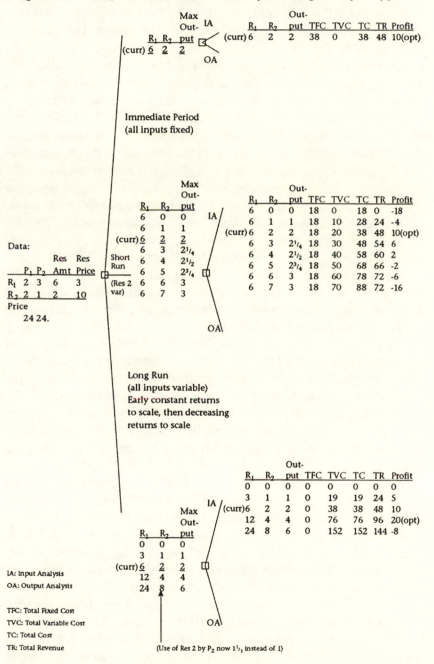

Max
Out-
R₁ R₂ put
(curr) 6 2 2

	R₁	R₂	Out-put	TFC	TVC	TC	TR	Profit
(curr)	6	2	2	38	0	38	48	10(opt)

IA

OA

Immediate Period
(all inputs fixed)

Max
Out-
R₁	R₂	put
6	0	0
6	1	1
(curr) 6	2	2
6	3	2¼
6	4	2½
6	5	2¾
(Res 2 6	6	3
var) 6	7	3

Short
Run

IA

	R₁	R₂	Out-put	TFC	TVC	TC	TR	Profit
	6	0	0	18	0	18	0	-18
	6	1	1	18	10	28	24	-4
(curr)	6	2	2	18	20	38	48	10(opt)
	6	3	2¼	18	30	48	54	6
	6	4	2½	18	40	58	60	2
	6	5	2¾	18	50	68	66	-2
	6	6	3	18	60	78	72	-6
	6	7	3	18	70	88	72	-16

Data:

	Res	Res		
	P₁	P₂	Amt	Price
R₁	2	3	6	3
R₂	2	1	2	10

Price
24 24.

OA

Long Run
(all inputs variable)
Early constant returns
to scale, then decreasing
returns to scale

	R₁	R₂	Out-put	TFC	TVC	TC	TR	Profit
	0	0	0	0	0	0	0	0
	3	1	1	0	19	19	24	5
(curr)	6	2	2	0	38	38	48	10
	12	4	4	0	76	76	96	20(opt)
	24	8	6	0	152	152	144	-8

IA

Max
Out-
R₁	R₂	put
0	0	0
3	1	1
(curr) 6	2	2
12	4	4
24	8	6

OA

IA: Input Analysis
OA: Output Analysis

TFC: Total Fixed Cost
TVC: Total Variable Cost
TC: Total Cost
TR: Total Revenue

(Use of Res 2 by P₂ now 1⅓ instead of 1)

Resource 2 is fixed at 2 hours, meaning a commitment of 2 hours has been made at $10 per hour. At the bottom of the data table we show that a product price of $24 per unit can be obtained whether it is produced by Process 1 or by Process 2.

Again, let us be aware that practical problems involve numerous and much larger input amounts, but our purpose here is to illustrate as simply as possible the methods that extend to large practical problems.

In Diagram 5.1 the first decision point (at the left) represents the choice of analyzing further the data for each of the three time periods (the immediate period, the short run, or the long run). The physical data from Diagram 4.1 are repeated but in each period another decision point appears (to the right) representing two types of analysis possible when the prices of the resource inputs and the product output are to be incorporated.

One type of analysis (the "input analysis," IA) is undertaken in Diagram 5.1 and focuses upon cost, revenue, and profit associated with varying Resource 2 amounts, while the Resource 1 amount remains fixed at 6.

The other type of analysis (the "output analysis," OA), to be illustrated in the following chapter, focuses upon cost, revenue, and profit associated with different product output amounts. Each approach makes a special contribution to decision making and economic analysis.

A very important lesson is to be learned in these two chapters. It is this: The optimal profit level of operation of the firm can be analyzed using *either* analysis. And the appropriate levels of *both* output and inputs that result in the optimal profit are revealed by either analysis.

Following the input analysis branches (IA) in Diagram 5.1, we see for each set of resource inputs specified in the decision period their maximum product output, their total fixed cost, their total variable cost, their total revenue from the output, and, finally, their total profit.

Very explicitly, these tables show the optimal profit level of resource inputs as well as its associated output. In the immediate period (top of Diagram 5.1) both inputs are fixed. The Resource 1 input at 6, with a price of $3, incurs a fixed cost of $18 and the Resource 2 input at 2, with a price of $10, incurs a fixed cost of $20. Thus, in the immediate period, total fixed cost of the inputs is $38 and because no inputs can be varied, there are no variable costs, so total costs are also $38. Because maximum product output is 2 units, and a price of $24 attained, total revenue is $48. Consequently, total profit is $10 ($48 − $38 = $10).

Contemplating the short-run period (middle of Diagram 5.1) and using the input analysis in Diagram 5.1, we see that the Resource 2 input of labor hours can be varied and eight different consequences are presented. Resource 2 cost is now viewed as a variable cost as different amounts of it may be obtained in the decision period.

For this firm, it turns out that in the short run the current Resource 1 and Resource 2 inputs of 6 and 2, with an output of 2, are still the most profitable even when Resource 2 could be varied. Thus, in the short run, with the current prices of the inputs and outputs holding fast, the optimal profit is $10.

As we view the long run (bottom of Diagram 5.1), the total situation changes as all of the inputs may be varied. In this example we have early constant returns to scale, so as we increase all inputs (in that range) by 100 percent increments and output increases by 100 percent, total costs also increase by 100 percent. In this range, doubling the output doubles total revenue, thus permitting total profit to double from its current $10 to $20.

Then, we assume *decreasing returns to scale* in the next 100 percent increment, so it is no surprise to see total profits decrease to a negative amount (–$8, which represents a loss of $8). Because output did not double in this range, total revenue did not double; and because total costs doubled, total profit fell. Therefore, considering our chosen increments, profit is maximized in the long run by committing to the Resource 1 and Resource 2 inputs of 12 and 4, respectively, which produce a profit of $20.

In our long-run analysis, all costs become variable and no fixed costs remain. The actual returns to scale that a given firm will experience as it increases its size are usually quite uncertain.

Problems

5.1   For the firm making furniture in Problem 4.1 we now incorporate the cost of the resource inputs and the price per unit of output. The following extended data table is now developed.

	Process 1	Process 2	Resource amount available	Resource price
Resource 1 (machine hours)	2 hours	4 hours	8 hours	$9
Resource 2 (labor hours)	3 hours	1 hour	2 hours	$11
Product price	$60	$60		

(a) As in Diagram 5.1, form a diagram for this firm focusing mainly on the input analysis in the short run. Include the maximum output table from Problem 4.1. If Problem 4.1 was not done, obtain graphically now the maximum output amounts for the immediate period and also for the short run when Resource 2 (labor hours) can be varied from 0 to 13 in whole-number amounts.

(b) For the immediate period when no inputs can be varied, complete a cost, revenue, and profit table. What is the optimal total profit amount?

(c) For the short-run analysis as Resource 2 (labor hours) is varied, complete a table showing cost, revenue, and profits for whole-number amounts of Resource 2.

(d) With Resource 2 variable, what is the optimal total profit amount?

(e) From the table in (c), what is the optimal amount of Resource 2 (labor hours) to hire in the short run, that is, the amount of Resource 2 that maximizes total profit?

(f) Is the current amount of Resource 2 the same as the optimal amount in the short run in (e) when it can be varied?

5.2 A firm making automobile parts was examined in Problem 4.2. The costs of the resource inputs and the price per unit of output are now shown in the following data table.

	Process 1	Process 2	Resource amount available	Resource price
Resource 1 (machine hours)	4 hours	2 hours	12 hours	$4
Resource 2 (labor hours)	1 hour	2 hours	6 hours	$13
Product price	$48	$48		

(a) Form a diagram for this firm, such as in Diagram 5.1, focusing mainly on the input analysis. Repeat the maximum output table from Problem 4.2, or generate it now for the immediate period when no inputs can change and for the short run when Resource 2 (labor hours) can be varied from 0 to 13 by whole-number amounts.

(b) For the immediate period, what is the optimal total profit amount?

(c) As in Diagram 5.1, complete a short-run cost, revenue, and profit table as Resource 2 (labor hours) is varied by whole-number amounts from 0 to 13.

(d) What is the optimal total profit amount as Resource 2 is varied?

(e) What is the optimal amount of Resource 2 (labor hours) as indicated in the table in (c)?

(f) Is the current amount of Resource 2 the same as the optimal amount in the short run when it can be varied?

5.3   The firm making shoes in Problem 4.3 faces a Resource 1 (machine hours) cost of $1 and a Resource 2 (labor hour) cost of $19. The product price per unit is $160.

(a) Form a diagram for this firm, such as in Diagram 5.1, focusing on the input analysis approach for the immediate period and the short run when Resource 2 (labor hours) can be varied by whole-number amounts. Use the maximum output data tables obtained in Problem 4.3 or generate them now by the graphical method.

(b) For the immediate period, the cost, revenue, and profit table reveals an optimal total profit of what amount?

(c) Extend the cost, revenue, and total profit analysis to the short-run period when Resource 2 (labor hours) can be varied. What is the optimal total profit amount?

(d) From the analysis in (c), what is the optimal amount of Resource 2 (labor hours) to hire?

(e) Is the current amount of Resource 2 the same as the optimal amount of Resource 2 in the short run when it can be varied?

5.4   The maker of backpacks in Problem 4.4 faces a product price per unit of $64. Resource 1 (machine hours) cost is $5 per hour and Resource 2 (labor hours) cost is $11 per hour.

(a) Construct a diagram for this firm as in Diagram 5.1 focusing on the input analysis approach. Use the maximum output data from Problem 4.4 or generate it now graphically.

(b) For the immediate period, complete a cost, revenue, and profit table. What is the optimal total profit amount?

(c) For the short-run analysis, form a cost, revenue, and profit table. For this period, what is the optimal total profit amount?

(d) From the analysis in (c), what is the optimal amount of Resource 2 (labor hours) to hire in the short run?

(e) Is the optimal amount of Resource 2 in the short run the same as the current amount of Resource 2?

6

Decision in the Firm: The Output Approach

As indicated in the previous chapter, the output analysis (OA) for decision making in the firm also yields the most profitable output as well as the inputs required to produce that output.

The output analysis appears in Diagram 6.1 and provides an extension of Diagram 5.1 of the previous chapter, which was limited to the input analysis (IA).

Diagram 6.1 brings together both types of analysis, showing in perhaps the simplest way how the optimal profit decision can be obtained by either analysis along with the associated resource inputs required and the total output.

The tables in Diagram 6.1 following the output-analysis branches are organized in such a way that whole-number output amounts appear first from the left and the required resource inputs appear next. Then, total fixed cost, total variable cost, total cost, total revenue, and total profit are connected to the output amounts rather than the input amounts, as in the input analysis. This permits us to proceed to useful graphical analysis of costs, revenue, and profit in the next chapter.

In the immediate period (top of Diagram 6.1), with resource inputs fixed, the only maximum output possibility is 2 units, and the one-line table shows optimal profit to be $10, as seen earlier in the input analysis as well.

In the short-run output analysis, however, four whole-number output possibilities are presented along with their costs, revenues, and profits (middle of Diagram 6.1). Here, again, we see the optimal profit to be $10, with an output of 2 units and Resource 1 and Resource 2 inputs of 6 and 2, respectively.

Diagram 6.1 Cost, Revenue, and Profit Analysis Extended to the Output Approach

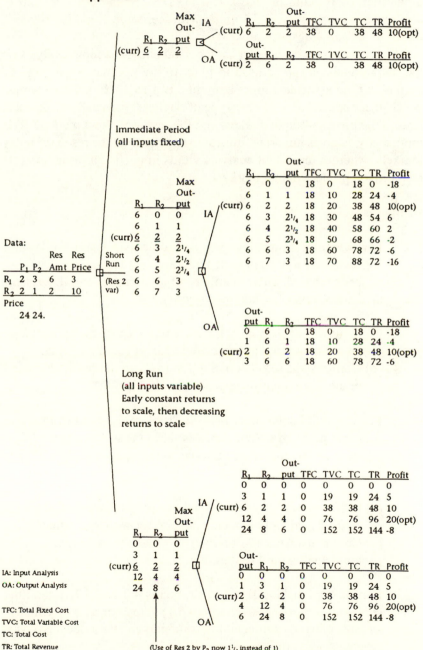

Data:

		Res	Res
	P_1 P_2	Amt	Price
R_1	2 3	6	3
R_2	2 1	2	10
Price			
	24 24.		

Immediate Period (all inputs fixed)

Short Run (Res 2 var)

Long Run (all inputs variable) Early constant returns to scale, then decreasing returns to scale

IA: Input Analysis
OA: Output Analysis

TFC: Total Fixed Cost
TVC: Total Variable Cost
TC: Total Cost
TR: Total Revenue

(Use of Res 2 by P_2 now $1^1/_2$ instead of 1)

In the long run, too, we see the same result as that obtained in the input analysis (bottom of Diagram 6.1). The optimal profit of $20 is associated with an output of 4 units, with Resource 1 and Resource 2 inputs of 12 and 4, respectively.

Thus, we see that for any decision period either the input analysis or the output analysis can be used to identify the optimal-profit level of output and the associated input amounts. But in the following chapter we shall see special uses of each type of analysis, especially as we look toward the product-output markets and the resource-input markets. The input analysis gives important information regarding the resource-input markets, whereas the output analysis yields important information relevant to the product-output markets.

Problems

6.1   For the furniture-making firm in Problems 4.1 and 5.1, extend the short-run analysis (as in Diagram 6.1) to include an output analysis table of whole-number output amounts and the associated costs, revenues, and total profits.

(a) In the output analysis of the short run, identify the optimal total profit amount and its associated total output of the product.

(b) Compare the results obtained in (a) with the results obtained in the input-analysis approach in Problem 5.1.

6.2   For the automobile parts firm in Problem 5.2 (and in Problem 4.2), construct an output analysis table (as in Diagram 6.1) for whole-number output amounts as Resource 2 (labor hours) is varied from 0 to 13 hours.

(a) In the short-run analysis when Resource 2 is varied, what are the optimal total profit amount and its associated total output?

(b) Compare the results obtained in (a) with those obtained in the input analysis in Problem 5.2.

6.3   For the firm making shoes in Problems 4.3 and 5.3, extend the short-run analysis (as in Diagram 6.1) to include an output analysis table of whole-number output amounts and the associated costs, revenues, and profits.

(a) From the short-run output analysis, what is the optimal total profit and its associated output?

(b) Compare the results obtained in (a) with those obtained in the input-analysis in Problem 5.3.

6.4 As in Diagram 6.1, extend the short-run analysis to include an output analysis with a table showing costs, revenues, and profits for whole-number amounts of Resource 2 (labor hours) for the maker of backpacks in Problems 4.4 and 5.4.

(a) From the short-run output analysis, what is the optimal total profit amount and its associated total output of the product?

(b) Compare the results obtained in (a) with the results obtained in the input-analysis approach in Problem 5.4.

7

Graphic Form for Product Supply and Resource Demand Analysis

In this chapter we develop a graphic representation of the optimal decision in the firm and discuss some of its benefits. And once again, we can see the optimal decision in terms of the input approach or the output approach.

Diagram 7.1 repeats the three decision periods confronting the firm along with much of the cost, revenue, and profit data from Diagram 6.1. However, in this chapter we construct relevant graphs and also explore the role of "marginal cost" and "marginal revenue" data in optimal decisions.

Graphic Input Analysis

Total cost and total revenue data for different levels of operations can be connected to variations either in terms of an input or the output. For the input analysis in Diagram 7.1 in the short run (middle of Diagram 7.1), we graph against the variable Resource 2 input total revenue (TR), total variable cost (TVC), and total cost (TC). Total fixed costs, being constant at $18, gives us a total cost graph that has the same slope of $10 as the total variable cost graph but is $18 higher.

We see again that in the short run the optimal Resource 2 input is 2 where total revenue exceeds total cost by the greatest amount, giving us again the maximum total profit of $10.

This total revenue graph typically will have breakpoints appearing due to the underlying diminishing marginal physical returns of the variable input, which we described in a previous chapter.

Diagram 7.1   The Graphic Form for Input and Output Analysis

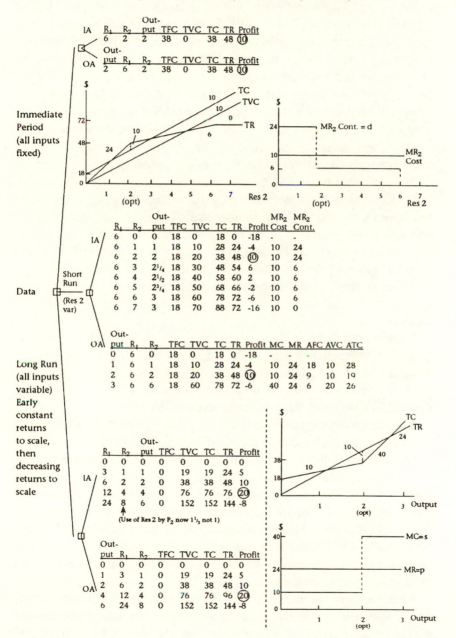

IA

R₁	R₂	Out-put	TFC	TVC	TC	TR	Profit
6	2	2	38	0	38	48	⑩

OA

Out-put	R₁	R₂	TFC	TVC	TC	TR	Profit
2	6	2	38	0	38	48	⑩

Immediate Period (all inputs fixed)

Short Run — IA (Data, Res 2 var)

R₁	R₂	Out-put	TFC	TVC	TC	TR	Profit	MR₂ Cost	MR₂ Cont.
6	0	0	18	0	18	0	-18	-	-
6	1	1	18	10	28	24	-4	10	24
6	2	2	18	20	38	48	⑩	10	24
6	3	2¼	18	30	48	54	6	10	6
6	4	2½	18	40	58	60	2	10	6
6	5	2¾	18	50	68	66	-2	10	6
6	6	3	18	60	78	72	-6	10	6
6	7	3	18	70	88	72	-16	10	0

OA

Out-put	R₁	R₂	TFC	TVC	TC	TR	Profit	MC	MR	AFC	AVC	ATC
0	6	0	18	0	18	0	-18	-	-	-		
1	6	1	18	10	28	24	-4	10	24	18	10	28
2	6	2	18	20	38	48	⑩	10	24	9	10	19
3	6	6	18	60	78	72	-6	40	24	6	20	26

Long Run (all inputs variable) Early constant returns to scale, then decreasing returns to scale

IA

R₁	R₂	Out-put	TFC	TVC	TC	TR	Profit
0	0	0	0	0	0	0	0
3	1	1	0	19	19	24	5
6	2	2	0	38	38	48	10
12	4	4	0	76	76	76	㉚
24	8	6	0	152	152	144	-8

(Use of Res 2 by P₂ now 1⅓ not 1)

OA

Out-put	R₁	R₂	TFC	TVC	TC	TR	Profit
0	0	0	0	0	0	0	0
1	3	1	0	19	19	24	5
2	6	2	0	38	38	48	10
4	12	4	0	76	76	96	㉚
6	24	8	0	152	152	144	-8

Alternatively, in the short-run analysis we can, in the output approach, graph TC and TR against output instead of against the variable resource input discussed above. This results in the breakpoints appearing now in the total cost graph, but again is due to the same underlying diminishing marginal physical returns of the variable input. Note that the total revenue graph has a constant slope now since we obtain a constant $24 per unit as more and more units of output are produced. But we see the optimal total profit of $10 again; now, however, it is associated with the output of 2 units. Also, at the output of 2, total revenue exceeds total cost by the greatest amount. The shapes of the graphs associated with the two approaches differ, but both graphic representations indicate the maximum total profit of $10.

In discussing the short-run analysis, we have made reference to breakpoints and slopes in the total revenue graph in the input analysis, and also in the total cost graph in the output analysis. It turns out that there is an equivalence between these slopes and "marginal contributions to total revenue" or "marginal contributions to total cost."

To show these marginal contributions to total revenue and to total cost we make the computations explicit in the corresponding tables in Diagram 7.1.

Looking at the input analysis (IA) first, we compute the increase in total cost for each additional unit of Resource 2. Because the price is $10 for each unit of Resource 2, the marginal Resource 2 cost (MR_2 Cost) is constant at $10. And thus the graph of the marginal Resource 2 cost (MR_2 Cost) gives us a constant straight line.

The last column in the table using the input approach shows the marginal contribution to total revenue of Resource 2 (MR_2 Cont.) to be constant at $24 when the marginal physical contribution of Resource 2 is 1 unit of output, but falls to $6 when the marginal physical product falls to ¼ unit. This continues through the Resource 2 input of 6. But as Resource 2 is increased beyond 6, the marginal contribution to total revenue of Resource 2 falls to $0, owing to the marginal physical contribution falling to 0 units of output. [*Note:* the marginal contribution to total revenue of a resource input is also known as the "marginal revenue product" of that resource as it is varied.]

Because there are usually only a limited number of processes available to the firm by which to produce the output, the "marginal contribution to revenue" graph of a variable resource input will be comprised of a series of steps due to the underlying shifts in the optimal use of combinations of the processes as a resource input is varied. We see in the example depicted in Diagram 7.1 that as more of Resource 2 is added, while Resource 1 (machine hours) remains fixed, the additional revenue from the additional labor hours decreases as there is less machine time available to accompany the additional labor hours, making more "hand process" necessary and resulting in fewer additional units being produced and thus less additional revenue.

As one's intuition might suspect, a firm is not at its most profitable level of operation when at that point the marginal cost of a variable resource input is greater than its marginal contribution to revenue. Likewise, when the firm is at a level in which the marginal cost of a variable resource input is less than its marginal contribution to revenue, maximum profit is not attained. It turns out that maximum total profit is associated with the point where the marginal cost per unit of the variable input is equal to the marginal contribution to revenue of that variable resource.

For our example, we have in Diagram 7.1 a graphic depiction (top right) of the marginal contribution to revenue of Resource 2 (MR_2 Cont.) as Resource 2 is varied along with the associated marginal cost of Resource 2 (MR_2 Cost). The point where the two graphs intersect indicates on the horizontal axis the Resource 2 amount generating the maximum total profit. Although the amount of the maximum total profit is not shown in these graphs, we see that it occurs at a Resource 2 input of 2 just as our total cost and total revenue graphs had indicated in Diagram 7.1.

The marginal data tend to be very useful for at least two reasons. First, they provide a ready indicator as to whether or not a firm is at its maximum total-profit level of operation and thus suggest whether an increase or a decrease in the variable input is appropriate.

Second, the marginal contribution to revenue graph of a resource implicitly provides the firm's demand curve for that resource if its price were to vary over time. Currently, the Resource 2 price we have in our example is $10, but if it were to be higher or lower it could affect the optimal amount of its acquisition.

If the price of Resource 2 were to change, the current marginal resource cost graph (MR_2 Cost) would shift upward or downward. And, with the MR_2 contribution graph (MR_2 Cont.) remaining unchanged, we can see the maximum-profit points of intersection being traced out on the MR_2 contribution graph of Resource 2.

Were the price of Resource 2 to rise, 2 units of Resource 2 would continue to be acquired until its price reached $24. Above $24 none would be acquired. In contrast, if the Resource 2 price were to fall below $6, 6 units of Resource 2 would be acquired. Therefore, we also label the MR_2 contribution graph as the firm's demand curve *d* for Resource 2.

As with most demand curves, this one, too, is downsloping from left to right. Again, we see more being acquired as the price is lower. Then, looking toward the entire Resource 2 market in a competitive economy we see that the demand side of the entire Resource 2 market would be comprised of all such firms, some, perhaps, with different Resource 1 endowments, giving a total market demand graph somewhat smoother than those associated with each individual firm.

Graphic Output Analysis

The marginal data developed in the output analysis (OA) is also very useful. It provides a ready indicator to the firm as to whether or not the current level of output is generating the maximum total profit. The intersection of the *marginal revenue* (MR) and *marginal cost* (MC) curves graphed against *output* gives us on the horizontal axis the output where total profit is maximized (bottom right side of Diagram 7.1).

The prevailing price (p) of the product output provides a constant marginal revenue graph (MR), whereas the upsloping marginal cost graph (MC) owes its shape to the underlying diminishing marginal physical product of the variable input.

Because the optimal output decision is associated with the intersection of the two graphs we can see that, if over time the firm was to be confronted with different prices, the most profitable output at each price would be indicated by points of intersection with the marginal cost graph. Thus, the *product supply graph* of the firm would be traced out giving a graph *equivalent to the firm's marginal cost graph*. We indicate in Diagram 7.1 (bottom right side) the marginal cost graph to be equivalent to the firm's supply curve "s".

In a competitive economy many such firms would exist, and the entire market supply curve would be the result of summarizing all of the firms' individual supply curves, each firm's supply curve being indicated by its marginal cost graph against output.

In the long run, when all inputs may increase, attention shifts to the physical returns to scale and their consequences on costs. In our example in Diagram 7.1 (bottom left side) we have assumed, as seen in the tables, a range of early constant returns to scale, but eventually decreasing returns to scale are encountered.

As long as constant returns to scale prevail, the firm's total profits increase by increasing the scale up to an output of 4 units. But beyond that output, decreasing physical returns to scale occur because of an increase from 1 hour to $1^{1}/_{3}$ hours in the rate of use of Resource 2 (labor hours) per unit of output by Process 2.

In real operations a question of vital concern, and one not usually easy to answer, is this: What will the physical returns to scale be if the scale is increased?

Problems

7.1 As in the example in Diagram 7.1, focus on the short-run analysis for the furniture-making firm as was done in Problem 6.1.

(a) Extend the input-analysis table from Problem 6.1 to include, for each whole-number amount of Resource 2, the marginal cost of each unit of Resource 2 (MR_2 Cost) and also the marginal contribution of each whole-number amount of Resource 2 (MR_2 Cont.).

(b) As in Diagram 7.1 construct from the table in (a) the following: graphs on total variable cost, total cost, and total revenue for the short-run problem (with variable Resource 2 amounts on the horizontal axis).

(c) Indicate on the graphs in (b) the optimal amount of Resource 2 to hire and the associated optimal total profit amount.

(d) Is the total profit before fixed costs but including total variable costs (TPBFC) maximized at the same Resource 2 input that maximizes total profit after fixed costs (TPAFC)? Indicate the amount of each and explain your answer.

(e) Now, as was done in Diagram 7.1, construct another graph of the problem. This time, from the slopes and breakpoints of the total cost and total revenue graphs in (b), plot the straight-line graph of the marginal cost of Resource 2 (MR_2 Cost) and the steps of the graph of the marginal contribution of Resource 2 (MR_2 Cont.), both against variable amounts of Resource 2 represented on the horizontal axis. Note the correspondence of the breakpoints in the total revenue graph with the ends of steps in the marginal resource contribution graph. Compare the results with those obtained in the table generated in (a).

(f) Observing the intersection of the marginal resource cost and marginal resource contribution graphs obtained in (e) and dropping down to the horizontal axis of Resource 2 amounts, we see again the optimal amount of Resource 2 as revealed in (c). What is this optimal amount of Resource 2 to hire? Explain why one unit more or one unit less of Resource 2 would not result in a higher total profit.

(g) As was done in Diagram 7.1, extend the output analysis table for the furniture maker that was obtained in Problem 6.1. Now include for all relevant whole-number outputs the marginal cost of output (MC); the marginal revenue of output (MR); the average fixed costs (AFC), that is, the fixed costs per unit of output; average variable costs (AVC), which also can be called the "variable costs per unit of output"; and the average total costs (ATC), also known as "total costs per unit of output." Each measure can have special uses.

(h) Graph against various output amounts the total costs and total revenues for the problem represented in the table in (g). From the graph identify the output associated with the maximum total profit amount. Note the correspondence of the optimal total profit amount and the optimal output amount obtained from the graph with that obtained in the table in (g).

(i) Now graph for this firm the marginal cost and marginal revenue of output as was done in Diagram 7.1. From the slopes and breakpoints of the total cost and total revenue graphs obtained in (h), create a graph of the steps of the marginal cost of output (MC) graph and the straight-line graph of the marginal revenue of output (MR). Dropping down from the intersection of the MC and MR graphs identifies the optimal output that generates the largest total profit. Explain why one more unit of output or one less would not result in any higher total profit.

7.2 For the automobile parts maker in Problem 6.2 we now need to extend the analysis of it such as that which was asked for regarding the furniture-making firm in Problem 7.1. For the automobile parts firm we are now asked to respond to the same requests as those that appeared in Problem 7.1 (a) through (i).

7.3   The data for the maker of shoes in Problem 6.3 can be analyzed further as was done for the furniture firm in Problem 7.1. For the shoe-making firm, too, respond to the same questions that were raised in Problem 7.1 (a) through (i).

7.4   Backpacks are made by one of our firms, and data for it was developed in Problems 4.4, 5.4, and 6.4. Now extend the analysis for this firm such as that which was requested for the furniture-making firm in Problem 7.1. Answer questions 7.1 (a) through (i), which pertain to the backpack-making firm.

Part II

Computational Economics and Decisions

8

The Practical Form for Decision:
Linear Programming

In previous chapters we focused on a simple example of a firm and observed the main elements and relationships that need to be taken into account for optimal decision in the firm.

In chapter 4 two processes were considered by which to make a product (jackets). One of the processes was a "hand process" that used labor heavily; the other was a "mechanized process" that made more use of sewing machines. Furthermore, only two resource inputs were involved: hours of labor and sewing machine hours.

We showed the need to use the resources efficiently by getting the most output from different possible amounts of the resource inputs and a recognition of the ever-present law of diminishing marginal physical returns related to additions of a single resource input, such as labor hours, when the amount of the other input (or inputs), such as machine hours, remains the same.

Then, when we attached costs to the inputs and revenue to the output we were able to identify the most profitable output under three different time periods: (1) the "immediate period" where no changes in inputs were possible; (2) the "short run" where one resource input (labor hours) could be varied; and, (3) the "long run" where all resource inputs could be varied.

By using the table-method in the previous chapters we were able, in this small example, to identify the optimal decision for each of the time periods. And doing this gave us a beginning in understanding the larger, more complex decisions one faces in real situations where many processes, many products, and many resource inputs are typically involved.

Fortunately, for the big realistic problems, modern mathematics, along with easy-to-use personal computer software, has provided us with a way to represent and solve such problems in a very straightforward way that requires very little background for the user.

The method is usually referred to as *linear programming.* The term "linear" essentially comes from the existence of the many straight-line relations, while the term "programming" pertains to the analysis and identification of an optimal decision or "program."

Let us now take the simple example from the previous chapters and illustrate the way the linear-programming method represents the situation and identifies the very same optimal decisions. Linear programming methods extend to solving large, vast problems that cannot be solved by the earlier procedures.

Again, we start with the same basic data table of the firm, which appears at the extreme left side of Diagram 8.1.

As we showed in earlier chapters, each row of the data tables represents a different resource and its rate of use by each of the processes along with the amount of that resource that is available. Clearly, we have to represent the limitation on output due to the limited amount of each resource that is available.

The step we take in linear programming to do this is to represent each resource row by a separate equality or "less-than" inequality. That means that the left-hand side, representing total usage of the resource by various programs, must be equal to, or less-than, the right-hand-side value, which represents the resource amount that is available.

Thus, we start by representing on the left-hand-side of each inequality various outputs of each process by a separate variable. The usual procedure uses X_1 to represent output by Process 1 (the hand process in our example) and X_2 the output by Process 2 (the machine process).

Thus, when we look at the Resource 1 row in the data table of Diagram 8.1, we take the rates of use of Resource 1 (machine hours) by each process (2 hours by the hand process, Process 1, and 3 hours by the mechanized process, Process 2) and assign each rate of use as a coefficient to the appropriate variables representing various amounts of product output by that process.

We see from the data table that, because 2 machine hours are required by Process 1, any output by Process 1 will be multiplied by 2 hours. Thus, we have $2X_1$ showing the total usage of Resource 1 for various outputs by Process 1.

Diagram 8.1 Linear Programming Form for Graphical Analysis and Optimal Decision

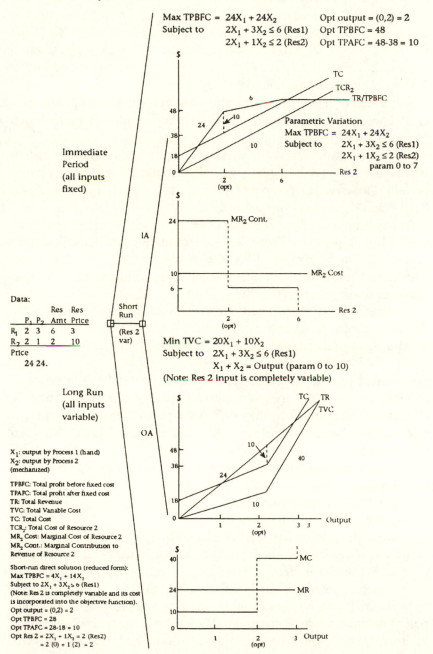

Max TPBFC = $24X_1 + 24X_2$ Opt output = (0,2) = 2
Subject to $2X_1 + 3X_2 \leq 6$ (Res1)   Opt TPBFC = 48
$2X_1 + 1X_2 \leq 2$ (Res2)   Opt TPAFC = 48-38 = 10

Parametric Variation
Max TPBFC = $24X_1 + 24X_2$
Subject to $2X_1 + 3X_2 \leq 6$ (Res1)
$2X_1 + 1X_2 \leq 2$ (Res2)
param 0 to 7

Immediate
Period
(all inputs
fixed)

IA

Data:

	Res	Res	
P_1 P_2	Amt	Price	
R_1 2 3	6	3	
R_2 2 1	2	10	
Price			
24 24.			

Short
Run
(Res 2
var)

Min TVC = $20X_1 + 10X_2$
Subject to $2X_1 + 3X_2 \leq 6$ (Res1)
$X_1 + X_2$ = Output (param 0 to 10)
(Note: Res 2 input is completely variable)

Long Run
(all inputs
variable)

OA

X_1: output by Process 1 (hand)
X_2: output by Process 2
(mechanized)

TPBFC: Total profit before fixed cost
TPAFC: Total profit after fixed cost
TR: Total Revenue
TVC: Total Variable Cost
TC: Total Cost
TCR_2: Total Cost of Resource 2
MR_2 Cost: Marginal Cost of Resource 2
MR_2 Cont.: Marginal Contribution to
Revenue of Resource 2

Short-run direct solution (reduced form):
Max TPBFC = $4X_1 + 14X_2$
Subject to $2X_1 + 3X_2 \leq 6$ (Res1)
(Note: Res 2 is completely variable and its cost
is incorporated into the objective function).
Opt output = (0,2) = 2
Opt TPBFC = 28
Opt TPAFC = 28-18 = 10
Opt Res 2 = $2X_1 + 1X_2 = 2$ (Res2)
= 2 (0) + 1 (2) = 2

Output by Process 2 requires 3 machine hours, so the output by that process, X_2, will have a coefficient of 3.

Total usage of Resource 1 (machine hours) by various output programs by both Process 1 and Process 2 involves the summation of the following: $2X_1 + 3X_2 = $ total Resource 1 required. For example, producing one unit of output by each process would require 5 machine hours: $2(1) + 3(1) = 5$ machine hours.

But ahead of time we do not know how much is best to produce by each process, and, of course, that is why we represent the output of each process by a variable.

In advance, however, we may know how much of each resource that will be available (or how much we might make available for a future period). These resource amounts from the data table become the right-hand-side values of our inequalities.

In our simple example, our data table indicates that we have 6 units of Resource 1 available. Therefore, our Resource 1 row in the data table gives us the inequality: $2X_1 + 3X_2 \leq 6$ machine hours. All values of X_1 and X_2 that result in total usage of Resource 1 amounts equal to 6, or less than 6, are therefore feasible.

Each resource row is handled similarly. In our example, the Resource 2 row pertaining to labor hours becomes: $2X_1 + 1X_2 \leq 2$ labor hours. Total usage of labor hours for the immediate period cannot exceed 2 hours.

We often refer to the entire set of inequalities as "the constraints." Here we have just two, the machine hour constraint and the labor hour constraint. Taken together, they define the set of "feasible programs," that is, those that are possible in light of the resource availabilities and their rates of use by the processes.

Thus, in our small example we have just the two following constraints expressed as "less-than" inequalities:

$2X_1 + 3X_2 \leq 6$ (machine hours)
$2X_1 + 1X_2 \leq 2$ (labor hours)

And graphing these inequalities gives us a graphic depiction of the set of feasible programs. The X_1 values (output by the hand process) are represented on the horizontal axis, and X_2 values (output by the machine process) are represented on the vertical axis.

In Figure 8.1 we construct such a graph by first plotting the *equation* part of the machine-hour constraint. By setting X_2 to zero we obtain the X_1 intercept of 3. And returning to the constraint and setting X_1 to zero,

Figure 8.1 **Graphical Approach to Identifying the Optimal Feasible Program in the Immediate Period With Both Resource Inputs Fixed**

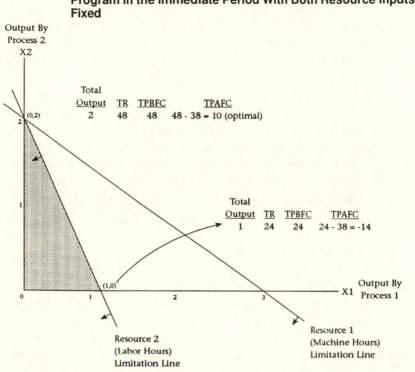

we obtain the X_2 intercept of 2. By connecting the two intercept points we obtain the Resource 1 "limitation line." Because Resource 1 is represented by an inequality, we indicate with small arrows that any programs that lie inside the limitation line are feasible, as well as those lying on the line, in terms of that resource.

Similarly, we find the intercepts for the labor-hour constraint inequality, Resource 2. Connecting these intercepts gives us a separate Resource 2 "limitation line" for labor hours.

Programs are not feasible if they lie beyond *either* the Resource 1 limitation line or the Resource 2 limitation line. In Figure 8.1 we shade the area representing the set of feasible programs—that is, the values of X_1 and X_2 that satisfy *both* inequality constraints.

But which of these many feasible programs of output is the most profitable in the "immediate period" when no changes can be made in the resource availabilities?

Importantly, it turns out that the most profitable program will lie at one of the *corner points* of the feasible region, which, for the immediate period, we have shaded in Figure 8.1. There, we have recorded at each corner point a number of items of importance: the output by each process; the total output by both processes; the total revenue (TR); the "total profit before fixed cost" (TPBFC); and the "total profit after fixed costs" (TPAFC).

The TPBFC is defined as TR minus TVC (total variable cost). Because in our example for the immediate period there are no variable costs (all costs are fixed), TR is simply equal to TPBFC.

Generally, however, our procedure (and the software using it) seeks to find the program that maximizes TPBFC *even when it is not equal to TR*. (The linearity of the objective function is still preserved.)

In later formulations we shall incorporate variable costs into the analysis but still seek the program that maximizes TPBFC. That program will also maximize TPAFC because the TPBFC of all feasible programs will require that the same fixed costs be subtracted.

Thus, the program with the maximum TPBFC is the program with the maximum TPAFC. Of course, once the maximum TPBFC is obtained we need to remember to subtract the total fixed costs from it to get the TPAFC. And maximizing TPAFC is usually our ultimate criterion.

For our example in Figure 8.1 we see that the (0,2) program has the maximum TPBFC of $48 compared to the other corner-point program, the (1,0) program, which has a TPBFC of $24.

Then, if the fixed cost of $38 is subtracted from the TPBFC of each corner-point program we see that the (0,2) program wins out with a TPAFC of $10, whereas the (1,0) program has a TPAFC of –$14 (a loss of $14). So all that is needed is to find the program that maximizes TPBFC, and, then, from the maximum TPBFC simply subtract the fixed cost from it alone and no others. And, of course, this aspect of the procedure extends to large problems where we use the software.

As seen at the extreme top of Diagram 8.1 we represent our small problem for the immediate period with an "objective function" along with the resource constraints.

The objective function is simply an equation that provides the TPBFC for each program. Of course, as we solve the problem we seek the feasible program that has the maximum TPBFC.

The TPBFC equation sums the unit profit before fixed cost for each process multiplied by the associated output by each process. For each process the unit profit amount is simply the unit revenue (usually the product price) less any unit variable cost of that process. But in this instance of the immediate period where no variable costs exist at all, the unit profit before fixed cost is simply equal to $24 for every process (the unit revenue or product price). Thus, the coefficients in our objective function in the immediate period will all be $24.

In summary, we say that we maximize the value of the objective function subject to satisfying all of the resource constraints that define the feasible region. For our small example, the solution procedure can be very simple: From a graph of the problem simply substitute each corner-point program of the feasible region into the objective function and identify the maximum. Naturally, it will be TPBFC, so from it we will need to subtract the total fixed costs, which, in a sense, have been set aside for the moment. This last step is necessary in problems of any size.

In larger problems with many processes, resources, and products, we need the procedure from modern mathematics, known as the *simplex method*, which is incorporated into popular software programs such as LINDO, developed by Linus Schrage of the University of Chicago. In the following sections of this chapter we shall see how to use the LINDO/PC version even though we may not have worked out the problem on our own by the simplex method. [*Note:* A discussion of the simplex method and illustrations of the solution procedure appear in my books *Linear Programming* (Macmillan 1971), and *Management Science* (McGraw-Hill 1976). Also see Linus Schrage, *LINDO: An Optimization Modeling System* (Scientific Press 1991).]

Entering the Problem Using LINDO/PC

Let us illustrate how we can use the LINDO software to solve the same problem that we solved graphically in Figure 8.1. Of course, for larger problems we would not have the opportunity for a graphical solution.

Analyzing the problem in the immediate period, we begin by focusing on the linear programming formulation at the top of Diagram 8.1. In that form we can enter it to be solved by the LINDO software.

Table 8.1 shows the steps involved in using the LINDO/PC software in solving our simple problem after inserting the LINDO/PC disk.

When "A>" appears, we enter the command LINDO on the same line. The response LINDO/PC will appear on the next line.

On the following line the colon symbol ":" appears, which is the sig-

---

Table 8.1

Entering the Problem Using the LINDO/PC Software Program

A > LINDO
: MAX 24X1+24X2
? ST
? 2X1+3X2<6
? 2X1+1X2<2
? END
: LOOK ALL

MAX 24X1+24X2
SUBJECT TO
        2) 2X1+3X2≤6
        3) 2X1+X2≤2
END

---

nal to enter the problem, line by line, beginning with the objective function on that same line.

After entering the objective function, preceded by MAX (or sometimes it could be MIN) and leaving TPBFC implicit, the question mark symbol "?" appears on the next line and that symbol starts every remaining line of the problem. On this line, following the objective function, we enter ST, which stands for "subject to."

Then, the constraints are entered, each on a separate line until all are entered. The "less than" symbol (<) will be interpreted as a "less than or equal to" symbol. After the last constraint, we enter the command END on a separate line.

After END is entered to indicate the end of the problem, a colon ":" appears on the next line, which permits us to enter the command LOOK ALL. This command allows a check to be made on the accuracy of the data entered; it also gives a number to each of the rows. The objective function is identified implicitly as Row 1, *the first constraint as Row 2*, *the second constraint as Row 3*, and so forth. In our example, we need to keep in mind that in this format our Resource 1 constraint (machine hours) is labeled as Row 2 and our Resource 2 constraint (labor hours) is referred to as Row 3.

Getting the Solution Using LINDO/PC

Once the problem has been entered and checked as in Table 8.1, we are ready to have the problem solved. And all that is necessary to obtain a

---

Table 8.2

Solving the Problem Using the LINDO/PC Software Program

```
: GO
         OBJECTIVE FUNCTION VALUE
1)       48.00
```

VARIABLE	VALUE	REDUCED COST
X1	.00	.00
X2	2.00	.00

ROW	SLACK OR SURPLUS	DUAL PRICES
2)	.00	6.00
3)	.00	6.00

DO RANGE (SENSITIVITY) ANALYSIS?
? NO

---

solution is to enter the command GO. The solution will then appear as shown in Table 8.2.

Row 1 in Table 8.2 will show the optimal value of the objective function. Recall that it is TPBFC and requires that, from it, fixed costs must be subtracted to obtain TPAFC.

Next, the optimal value of each of the X-variables appears showing the feasible output programs that will attain the maximum TPBFC value of $48. In our example, we see again that the optimal value of X_1 is 0 and X_2 is 2, that is, the (0,2) program.

The "reduced cost" column provides supplementary information for future planning, but may be of limited use at the moment. (The technical point is that the mathematical procedures in the software reveal how much each unit of profit in the objective function would have to improve before the associated variable could enter the optimal program with a positive value.)

The rest of the information revealed by the software in the solution section pertains to the constraints, particularly their right-hand sides, which here represent the resource amounts available.

Recalling that Row 2 in the LINDO solution format pertains to our Resource 1 (machine hours), we see that the "slack" in Resource 1 is zero, meaning all available machine hours would be used in the optimal program. From our graphical solution in Figure 8.1 we see, too, that the optimal program lies on the Resource 1 limitation line and has no unused amount.

Row 3 in Table 8.2 represents Resource 2 (labor hours) where the amount available is also fully used in the optimal (0,2) program and has a slack value of zero as well. The graphical solution shows the program lying on the Resource 2 limitation line, too.

The "dual" term, heading the remaining column, comes from the mathematics used in the software. Essentially, it refers to the surprising simultaneous determination of the optimal program of *output* and the "value" at the margin of each of the resource *inputs* represented in the constraints. Thus, when the optimal output program is obtained, *the value to the firm of another unit of each resource input (considered individually) is also revealed.*

Each of these resource-input values is sometimes referred to as a "price," because it would be profitable for the firm to pay up to that amount for additional units of the resource. Thus, we see the "dual price" revealed for each of the resources represented in the constraints. We see it to be $6 for Resource 1 (machine hours) and also $6 for Resource 2 (labor hours).

In earlier chapters we used the term "marginal contribution of Resource 1" and "marginal contribution of Resource 2" to refer to these same values. It is instructive to look back to Diagram 7.1 and note the equivalence of "the marginal contribution of Resource 2" with the "dual price" of Resource 2 (as shown in Row 3 in Table 8.2).

The last line that appears in Table 8.2 asks if the "range analysis" is to be undertaken. (It is also referred to as "sensitivity analysis.") While we say NO for the moment, this additional analysis may be very useful as we look beyond the immediate period. It will reveal the ranges of resource amounts over which the current marginal contributions (or "dual prices") will hold. This is very useful when one looks forward, in the "short run," to increasing or decreasing any one of the resource amounts by a *limited* amount. In Diagram 7.1, however, we undertook a more extensive variation of one of the resources, Resource 2. The results we obtained there, using graphs and tables, can be obtained also with the LINDO software, which permits our analysis to be extended to practical problems of great size. We shall discuss this option of the software next.

The Short-Run Decision

In the short run at least one of the resource inputs can be varied. In our small example we are able, in this time period, to vary the labor hour input (Resource 2) while the machine hour input (Resource 1) remains fixed at 6.

At this time, we want to vary Resource 2 extensively, not merely over a very limited range, as would be done in the "range analysis" option raised in Table 8.2. And in linear programming analysis there are two ways to study this *extensive* variation. One way, to be examined later, is to create a formulation by which we can obtain a *direct solution* of the optimal program as well as the associated Resource 2 input, which would be necessary to implement that program. This would be the quick way to solve the problem, but it does not provide the useful graphical insights of "parameterization."

When using the parametric approach, in effect, we see the Resource 2 input at different values and solve repeatedly, in a sense, for the optimal program with the different Resource 2 amounts. This approach has a number of advantages, as we shall see later. Most importantly, it shows explicitly how the costs and revenues behave as the input varies extensively, giving us useful insights for future decisions and optimal responses to possible changes in output prices or input costs.

Short-Run Analysis by Parameterization

We prepare for our parameterization procedures by first *altering the original* problem so that we can get a complete graph of the effect on TPBFC of the resource we wish to vary. Here we have focused on Resource 2 (labor hours).

We begin by setting the Resource 2 amount to zero so we can see what the TPBFC will be when there is none of the resource at all. Then, we will parameterize it until no changes in TPBFC occur.

Because our data table in Diagram 8.1 showed that Resource 2 is used in every process, it is no surprise that when we solve this altered problem, with Resource 2 at zero, the optimal TPBFC is zero.

How do we alter the original problem? As shown in Table 8.3, first enter the command LOOK ALL to review the original problem after we have solved the original problem and have indicated NO to the range analysis. Then enter the command ALTER as shown in Table 8.3. A request for the ROW to be altered will now appear, and because we are focusing on Resource 2, we will enter 3 (for Row 3, as that is the row number for Resource 2 in the format).

Next, the request will appear for the specific variable to be altered. In

---

Table 8.3

Altering the Original Problem by Setting the Resource 2 Amount to Zero in Order to Undertake an Extensive Analysis of Resource 2 Variation

```
: LOOK ALL
MAX 24X1 + 24X2
SUBJECT TO
        2) 2X1+3X2≤6
        3) 2X1+X2≤2
END
: ALTER
ROW:
3
VAR:
RHS
NEW COEFFICIENT:
? 0
: LOOK ALL

MAX 24X1+24X2
SUBJECT TO
        2) 2X1+3X2≤6
        3) 2X1+X2≤0
END
```

---

this instance, it is the right-hand side of Row 3, representing Resource 2, so we simply enter RHS. [*Note:* Technically, the right-hand-side values are usually not variables—they are constants—and they do not have coefficients; but the software is designed to allow coefficients of variables in the objective function and constraints to be altered when desired, thus the strained terminology as we alter the right-hand-side value.]

Next appearing will be a request for the NEW COEFFICIENT (as seen in Table 8.3). Zero is the value we assign because that is where we want to start. To verify this change, enter LOOK ALL and make the check to see whether the desired change was made.

Next, we enter GO to solve the altered problem. To no surprise we see it gives an optimal program of (0,0) and a TPBFC value of zero. This is shown in Table 8.4. (In larger problems, some processes may not use a specific resource input and thus the optimal program may have a TPBFC greater than zero, even when the resource input is zero.)

We say again NO to the range analysis, but we are now set to parameterize the Resource 2 amount from zero upward. To do so, we enter LOOK ALL and then the command PARA as shown in Table 8.5.

We are then asked for the ROW number (as seen in Table 8.5). It will

Table 8.4

The Optimal Solution When the Resource 2 Amount Is Altered and Set to Zero

```
: GO
          OBJECTIVE FUNCTION VALUE
1)        .00
```

VARIABLE	VALUE	REDUCED COST
X1	.00	24.00
X2	.00	.00

ROW	SLACK OR SURPLUS	DUAL PRICES
2)	6.00	.00
3)	.00	24.00

```
DO RANGE (SENSITIVITY) ANALYSIS?
? NO
```

Table 8.5

The Results of Parameterizing the Resource 2 Amount From Zero to 7

```
: LOOK ALL
MAX 24X1 + 24X2
SUBJECT TO
        2) 2X1+3X2≤6
        3) 2X1+X2≤0
END
: PARA
ROW:
3
NEW RHS VAL=
7
```

PIVOT ROW	RHS VAL	DUAL VARIABLE	OBJ VAL
2	2.00	24.00	48.00
3	6.00	6.00	72.00
0	6.00	.00	72.00

be 3, which identifies Resource 2 (labor hours). Next will be the request for the NEW RHS VALUE. This pertains to the upper limit we wish to set on Resource 2 in our analysis. Our familiarity with the problem suggests we set the limit at (say) 7 as any amount higher than that would likely be superfluous.

Table 8.6

A More Complete Table Showing the Results of Parameterizing Resource 2 From Zero to 7

RHS VAL (Res 2 amount at a breakpoint in the TPBFC graph)	DUAL VARIABLE (slope of TPBFC graph preceding breakpoint)	OBJ VAL (optimal value of TPBFC at breakpoint but does not include Res 2 costs—the resource being parameterized)
0	—	$ 0
2	$24	48
6	6	72
6 (representing Res 2 amounts beyond 6)	0	72

Quickly, we are presented with the results of a parameterization of Resource 2 amounts from zero up to 7. A table appears as in Table 8.5, showing slopes and breakpoints for the TPBFC graph we want to construct against Resource 2 amounts.

However, the table presented by the software (in Table 8.5), showing the result of parameterizing Resource 2, needs some elaboration.

The RHS VAL column that appears shows only the Resource 2 amounts where breakpoints in the TPBFC graph occur; the OBJ VAL column in Table 8.5 shows these TPBFC values at the breakpoints. The DUAL VARI- ABLE column depicts the slopes of the TPBFC graph (that is, the marginal contributions of Resource 2) *just preceding* each breakpoint.

From our earlier altered problem, we found the optimal TPBFC to be zero when Resource 2 was zero. We include this with the information from the software table in a more complete and elaborated table shown in Table 8.6.

We create in Figure 8.2 the TPBFC values against the Resource 2 amounts we are parameterizing. Recall that in such parameterization TPBFC does not take into account the total Resource 2 costs, which increase at the rate of $10 (because its price is $10).

Therefore, we need to include in Figure 8.2 the graph of the total cost of Resource 2 (TCR2) with a slope of $10. Then, adding to it the fixed cost of Resource 1, which is $18, gives us the desired total cost graph (TC).

As we saw before in Diagram 8.1, the optimal TPAFC of $10 is attained with a Resource 2 input of 2.

Figure 8.2   **Graphical Analysis of the Variation of Resource 2**

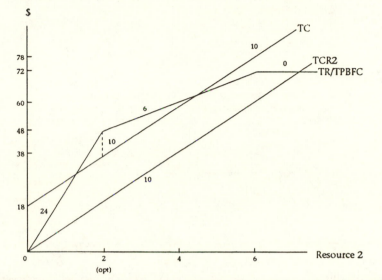

The optimal Resource 2 input of 2 hours is identified and the total profit after fixed cost of $10.

A graph of the marginal contribution of Resource 2, which is equal to the slopes of the TPBFC graph, appears in Figure 8.3. Then, plotting in Figure 8.3 the marginal Resource 2 cost (its price), as well, we observe again the optimal Resource 2 amount of 2 where the two graphs intersect.

Figure 8.3 shows in a very quick way the optimal amount of Resource 2 for the firm to acquire at *various* Resource 2 prices. Thus, we see why the marginal contribution graph in Figure 8.3 is spoken of as being equivalent to the graph of the demand for Resource 2 by the firm.

Then, if other firms in the Resource 2 (labor) market are similarly situated, technologically and in terms of other resources, insight into the entire Resource 2 market demand is provided by aggregating each firm's demand. And, given a market *supply* graph of Resource 2, future price changes in Resource 2 can be anticipated from possible shifts that might occur in the Resource 2 market supply curve.

Thus, we have used our simple problem to illustrate some of the uses of the parameterization in the analysis of large, practical problems.

But one step remains in our short-run analysis. It is the identification of the *optimal program of output by process* that would attain the TPAFC of $10 with a Resource 2 input of 2.

Figure 8.3 **Graphical Analysis of the Variation of Resource 2 Showing the Marginal Contribution of Resource 2 and the Marginal Cost of Resource 2**

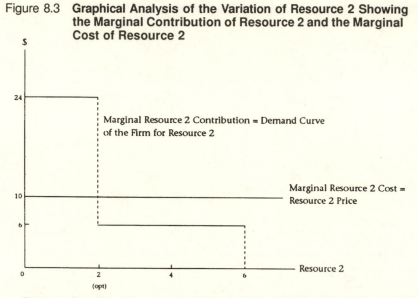

Because the optimal Resource 2 amount is indicated by the point of intersection, the firm's entire Resource 2 demand curve can be traced out for various possible Resource 2 prices.

All that is needed is re-formulation of the problem with the already determined optimal Resource 2 input of 2. In our example the Resource 2 input had been 2 in the immediate period, so it would simply be reset at 2, so to speak.

If we then solve the "re-formulated" problem below we obtain the optimal program of (0,2), meaning a total output of 2. As we said, it happens to be the very program that we found to be optimal in the immediate period in our earlier analysis using tables and graphs.

Max TPBFC = $24\,X_1 + 24\,X_2$
Subject to $\quad 2\,X_1 + 3\,X_2 \le 6$ (Resource 1)
$\quad\quad\quad\quad 2\,X_1 + 1\,X_2 \le 2$ (Resource 2)

Short-Run Analysis by Direct Solution

In this approach we create a single linear programming formulation as shown in the lower left-hand side of Diagram 8.1. We reach, of course, the same optimal program and Resource 2 input as in the parametric approach. Here, Resource 2 is assumed to be *completely* variable, with its cost being incorporated into the coefficients of the objective function.

Therefore, in specifying the coefficients of this formulation we need to identify the Resource 2 cost per unit of output by each process and subtract these unit variable costs from the unit revenue of that process.

The original data table in Diagram 8.1 provides the information needed. From it we see that a unit of output by Process 1 (the hand process) requires 2 hours of labor. And because Resource 2 costs $10 per hour, we find the Resource 2 costs per unit of output by Process 1 to be $20. This $20 is then subtracted from the unit revenue of $24, giving us a $4 unit profit before fixed costs in the short run when Resource 2 is completely variable.

By Process 2, only 1 hour of labor is used, so the Resource 2 variable cost per unit of output by that process is only $10, giving a unit profit (before fixed cost) of $14.

The linear programming formulation for the direct solution can then drop the Resource 2 constraint and maximize the modified objective function with the single Resource 1 constraint as follows:

Max TPBFC = $4 X_1 + 14 X_2$

Subject to $\quad 2 X_1 + 3 X_2 \leq 6$ (Resource 1).

For this problem a graphical solution is possible, as seen in Figure 8.4, and corresponds to our earlier solution. Of course, for large problems the direct solution of the reformulated problem cannot be solved graphically.

To identify the amount of Resource 2 that is needed to implement the direct solution we need to substitute the original (0,2) solution into the Resource 2 constraint (that we have set aside) as follows: $2 X_1 + 1 X_2 = 2(0) + 1(2) = 2$ hours of Resource 2. Note that the optimal program obtained and the required Resource 2 input correspond to the results obtained in the parametric approach.

Another Formulation That Focuses on the Product Output Supply Curve

As we noted in chapter 7, a quick way to assess the response of a firm to possible product price changes in the short run is to look at its marginal cost curve. We derived this curve in Diagram 7.1 when Resource 2 could be varied extensively but have not done so using a linear programming formulation.

To do this we generate the minimum total variable cost (TVC) at various output levels by parameterizing *total product output*. The linear

Figure 8.4   **Graphical Approach in Identifying the Optimal Feasible
Program in the Short Run by the Direct Method**

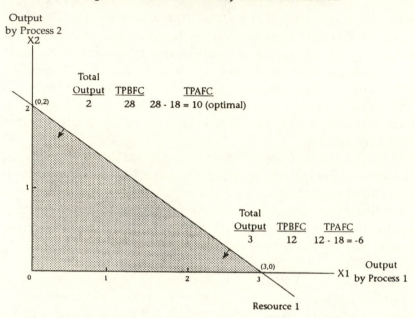

Resource 2 (labor hours) is completely variable and its costs are incorporated into the coefficients of the TPBFC objective function.

programming formulation appears in the middle of Diagram 8.1. The graph of TVC for various output amounts is shown in Figure 8.5.

The slopes of the total variable cost graph (TVC) obtained (the "dual prices") provide the marginal cost of output values. Using LINDO we obtain the results shown in Figures 8.5 and 8.6.

Because we are assuming only Resource 2 to be completely variable, the coefficients in the TVC objective function are simply the unit variable costs of Resource 2 by each of the processes.

From the data table in Diagram 8.1, we see the coefficient of X_1 (output by Process 1) will be $20 (2 times $10). It will be $10 (1 times $10) for X_2 (output by Process 2).

The Resource 1 constraint remains as before, but the Resource 2 constraint is dropped because its cost is incorporated into the objective function.

We need to obtain the minimum TVC for each output level in the relevant range. This we do by adding a product output equation con-

Figure 8.5 **Graphical Analysis of Total Variable Costs, Total Costs, and Total Revenue as Output Is Varied Due to Resource 2 Becoming Completely Variable**

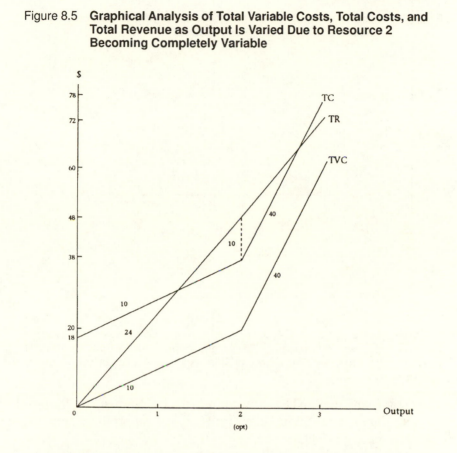

Optimal product output is seen to be 2 units where total profit after fixed costs is $10, the same as that found in the input analysis.

straint, which sums the output by all processes and parameterizes the total output from zero upward.

With the marginal cost graph obtained, we can observe in Figure 8.6 the optimal output at the intersection points with various possible prices (marginal revenues). Thus, we have the individual firm's product supply curve using LINDO.

Problems

8.1 From the data in Problem 5.1 regarding the furniture-making firm, place the problem for the immediate period in linear programming form as in Diagram 8.1.

Figure 8.6 **Graphical Analysis of the Effect of Varying Resource 2 on the Marginal Cost of Product Output**

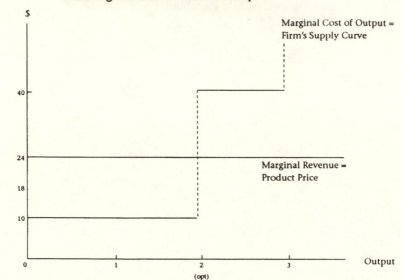

Given a product price of $24, the optimal output is shown to be 2 units at the point of intersection with the marginal revenue graph (which here is equal to the product price). Thus, the firm's entire product supply graph can be traced out for various possible prices.

(a) Using the LINDO software, what is the optimal feasible program in the immediate period and its total profit before fixed costs (TPBFC)?

(b) What is the optimal total profit after fixed costs (TPAFC)?

(c) As a first step in the parametric variation of the Resource 2 amount, alter the Resource 2 amount to zero, and solve the newly created problem in order to start developing a full graphic representation of its cost and profit consequences from zero upward. When Resource 2 amount is zero, what is the optimal program and its TPBFC? TPAFC?

(d) Parameterize the Resource 2 amount from 0 to 13 by invoking the PARA command in LINDO. The slopes and breakpoints of the total revenues (or TPBFC) graph against Resource 2 variation will be revealed. (Recall that the marginal contributions of Resource 2 will be called "dual prices" and are equivalent to the slopes.) Construct the TR/TPBFC graph for Resource 2 amounts from 0 to 13.

(e) To the TR/TPBFC graph developed in (d) add the total Resource 2 cost graph, which has a slope equal to its unit cost.
While the total Resource 2 cost increases as more of it is added
to the operation, the parameterization procedure, in effect,
treats it as being fixed at different Resource 2 input levels.
The total fixed cost of other resource inputs, here only Resource 1, is simply added to the Resource 2 total cost graph to
obtain the desired total cost graph. After doing this, what optimal Resource 2 is indicated and what is the optimal total
profit (TPAFC) amount? Compare this result with that obtained in Problems 5.1, 6.1, and 7.1.

(f) From the graphs generated in (e) plot the graphs of the marginal cost of Resource 2 (MR2 COST) and the marginal contribution of Resource 2 (MR2 CONT), both against Resource
2 amounts on the horizontal axis. Identify the optimal amount
of Resource 2 from these graphs and compare the results with
that obtained in (e).

(g) As seen in the example problem in Diagram 8.1, formulate
now for the furniture-making firm an output-analysis programming problem that minimizes an objective function comprised
of the variable cost per unit of product output by each process. Total variable cost (TVC) here includes only Resource 2
costs. The constraints include the fixed Resource 1 constraint
plus a total product output constraint, which is parameterized
from zero upward. The resulting TVC graph plotted against
total output along with the total revenue graph shows the optimal output and its total profit before the fixed cost of Resource 1. Add the fixed cost to your graph and compare the
optimal total profit obtained with that obtained in the input
analysis in (e).

(h) From the TC and TR graphs obtained in (g), produce the corresponding marginal cost and marginal revenue of output
graphs. Show how the point of intersection reveals the optimal total output. Compare the result with that obtained in (g).

(i) Now for the direct solution to the short-run problem when
Resource 2 (labor hours) is completely variable. Formulate
the new linear programming problem with the new coefficients in the objective function reflecting the cost per unit of
Resource 2 by each process. With the Resource 2 cost being

incorporated into the objective function, the Resource 2 constraint can be dropped. Solve by LINDO for the optimal program of product output, TPBFC, TPAFC, and the optimal amount of Resource 2 indicated by the optimal output program. Compare these results with those obtained in (c) through (e) and (g).

8.2 Place the data for the automobile parts firm in Problem 5.2 in linear programming form for the immediate period such as was asked regarding the furniture-making firm in Problem 8.1. For the automobile parts firm respond to the same requests as those that appeared in Problem 8.1 (a) through (i).

8.3 From the data for the shoe-making firm in Problem 5.3, develop for the immediate period the linear programming formulation as requested for the furniture-making firm in Problem 8.1. Then, respond to the same questions for this firm that were raised for the furniture firm in Problem 8.1 (a) through (i).

8.4 Backpacks are made by the firm in Problem 5.4. Now place that problem for the immediate period in linear programming form and respond to the questions raised in Problem 8.1 for the furniture firm as they pertain to the backpack firm in Problem 8.1 (a) through (i).

9

Changes in Product Price and Changes in Labor Cost

In this chapter we apply the analysis of the previous chapter and illustrate separately the effects on the firm of two common occurrences: (1) a change in the product price and (2) a change in a resource price, such as the labor cost per hour. Only one change at a time is assumed in our firm in order to trace its effects. We repeat the type of analysis shown in Diagram 8.1 of the previous chapter but under the changed conditions.

A Change in the Product Price

A change in the product price from $24 to $48 is the first change assumed. And this alters the coefficients in the objective function in the immediate period from 24 to 48.

The result in the immediate period is that, while no increase in product output is possible because all resource inputs are fixed, the optimal TPBFC increases from $48 to $96, and the TPAFC increases from $10 to $58.

For the short run under the higher product price, we see from the parameterization of the Resource 2 input and its resulting graphs, as shown in the input analysis (IA) section of Diagram 9.1, a sharp upward shift of the TPBFC graph. Its slopes, you recall, define the marginal contribution of Resource 2. Now, both graphs show that the optimal Resource 2 amount is 6 rather than 2.

At the higher Resource 2 input of 6, the TPBFC is $144 and the TPAFC is $66, clearly superior to the TPBFC of $96 (and the TPAFC of $58) at the former optimal Resource 2 input of 2.

Diagram 9.1   **Linear Programming Analysis of the Short Run Under a Product Price Increase**

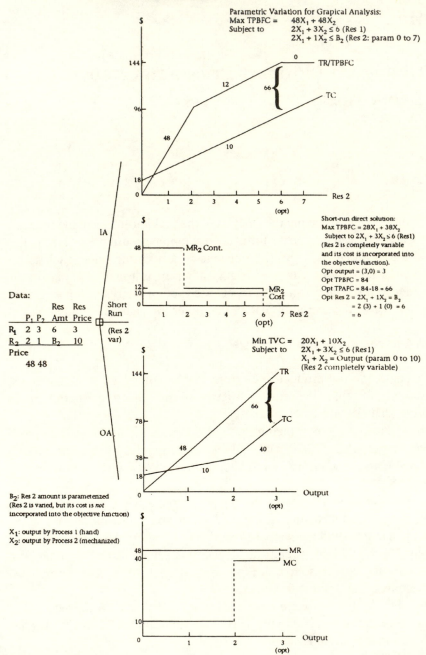

Parametric Variation for Grapical Analysis:

Max TPBFC = $48X_1 + 48X_2$

Subject to $2X_1 + 3X_2 \leq 6$ (Res 1)

$2X_1 + 1X_2 \leq B_2$ (Res 2: param 0 to 7)

Short-run direct solution:

Max TPBFC = $28X_1 + 38X_2$

Subject to $2X_1 + 3X_2 \leq 6$ (Res1)

(Res 2 is completely variable and its cost is incorporated into the objective function).

Opt output = (3,0) = 3

Opt TPBFC = 84

Opt TPAFC = 84-18 = 66

Opt Res 2 = $2X_1 + 1X_2 = B_2$

= 2 (3) + 1 (0) = 6

= 6

Data:

	Res P_1	Res P_2	Res Amt	Res Price
R_1	2	3	6	3
R_2	2	1	B_2	10
Price				
	48	48		

Short Run (Res 2 var)

IA

OA

Min TVC = $20X_1 + 10X_2$

Subject to $2X_1 + 3X_2 \leq 6$ (Res1)

$X_1 + X_2 = $ Output (param 0 to 10)

(Res 2 completely variable)

B_2: Res 2 amount is parameterized (Res 2 is varied, but its cost is *not* incorporated into the objective function)

X_1: output by Process 1 (hand)

X_2: output by Process 2 (mechanized)

We should note that the underlying marginal *physical product* of Resource 2 has not changed, including the point of diminishing marginal physical returns (it is at an input of 2). But the higher product price has increased the optimal amount of Resource 2 from 2 to 6. Thus, in the short run the optimal amount of Resource 2 for the firm is *not* at the point of diminishing marginal physical returns, but is beyond it.

Small increases in the product price may not have such a dramatic effect as in the case here, but such analysis would reveal the magnitude of the effect, if any. Of course we should be aware of the fact that we are still assuming that the Resource 2 price remains at $10.

From the short-run output analysis (OA) section of Diagram 9.1, we see the effect of the product price increase on total revenue and its slope. Clearly, the graphs in that section show the new optimal output to be 3 units (rather than 2).

The increase in product output in the short run in response to a higher product price is common in most markets, and in our example we are able to obtain the specific increase in the optimal output for our firm. The dynamics of competitive markets, however, are such that the higher product price may over time entice new firms to enter the industry (or existing ones to expand), thus tending to drive the price back down. The market price would tend to fall until it was equal to the average total cost of the product plus a necessary ("normal") profit per unit.

The short-run direct solution shown at the right-hand side in Diagram 9.1 reveals very quickly both the optimal output program (3,0) and the associated optimal Resource 2 input of 6.

It is interesting, too, to see how the product price increase has affected the use of the processes in the optimal program. Before the product price increase, it was optimal for all output to be produced by the mechanized Process 2. After the product price increase, it is optimal to produce all of the output by the labor-intensive Process 1.

A Change in a Resource Price

In this section we trace the effects of an increase in the hourly cost of labor (Resource 2) from $10 to $14. In doing this we return to the firm under the original technology and assume a product price of $48, as we did in Diagram 9.1.

In doing the parameterization of Resource 2 in the short-run input analysis, we see that the downsloping demand curve for a resource in-

---

Box 9.1

Minimum-Wage Legislation

In 1938 the Fair Labor Standards Act established in the United States a minimum wage that became applicable to most industries. Since then, upward revisions have been made periodically as price levels have risen. Debate continues, however, on its effects and its desirability regarding this approach to providing aid to lower-wage workers.

---

put appears here as it usually does and as we derived it in Diagram 9.1. We repeat it in Diagram 9.2 along with the new Resource 2 price of $14. From the original graph of the marginal contribution of Resource 2 in Diagram 9.1, we could have foreseen the optimal Resource 2 amount falling from 6 to 2 if the Resource 2 price were to rise from $10 to $14 and impose on the firm a new marginal Resource 2 cost of $14.

Diagram 9.2 shows a much fuller analysis of the Resource 2 price increase to $14. We see that the TPAFC now is at a maximum of $50 when the Resource 2 input is 2, and, also, that the optimal product output is 2 units.

The direct solution to the short-run problem (after the Resource 2 price increase) reveals the same optimal information as well as the optimal amount to be produced by each process. Now, all output is to be produced by the mechanized Process 2. The higher Resource 2 price has therefore resulted in a shift from all production by the labor-intensive Process 1 to the mechanized Process 2, with the accompanying reduction in the optimal Resource 2 input from 6 to 2.

Problems

9.1   (a) Consider a product-price change for the furniture firm analyzed in Problem 8.1 (first encountered in Problem 4.1). The product price has increased from $60 to $75. Under the new product price, respond, using LINDO, to the questions asked in Problem 8.1 (a) through (i). Discuss the impact of the product-price increase on the optimal output, the optimal output program, and the optimal TPBFC and TPAFC.

Diagram 9.2 Resource 2 Price Increase Under Original Technology: Short-Run Analysis

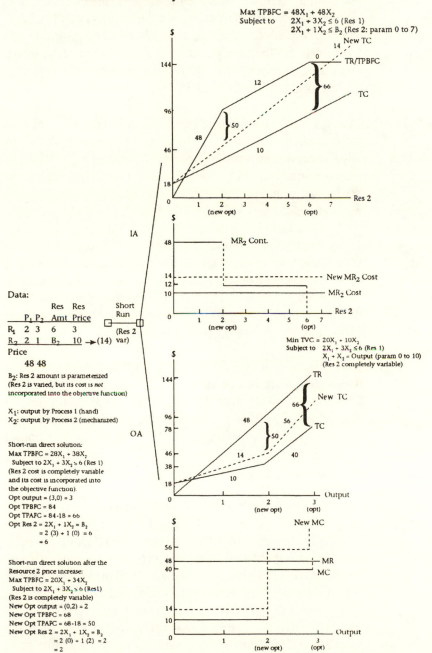

Max TPBFC = $48X_1 + 48X_2$
Subject to $2X_1 + 3X_2 \leq 6$ (Res 1)
  $2X_1 + 1X_2 \leq B_2$ (Res 2: param 0 to 7)

Data:

	Res	Res		Short
	P_1 P_2	Amt	Price	Run
R_1	2 3	6	3	(Res 2
R_2	2 1	B_2	10 →(14)	var)
Price				
	48 48			

B_2: Res 2 amount is parameterized
(Res 2 is varied, but its cost is *not*
incorporated into the objective function)

X_1: output by Process 1 (hand)
X_2: output by Process 2 (mechanized)

Short-run direct solution:
Max TPBFC = $28X_1 + 38X_2$
  Subject to $2X_1 + 3X_2 \leq 6$ (Res 1)
(Res 2 cost is completely variable
and its cost is incorporated into
the objective function).
Opt output = (3,0) = 3
Opt TPBFC = 84
Opt TPAFC = 84-18 = 66
Opt Res 2 = $2X_1 + 1X_2 = B_2$
  = 2 (3) + 1 (0) = 6
  = 6

Short-run direct solution after the
Resource 2 price increase:
Max TPBFC = $20X_1 + 34X_2$
  Subject to $2X_1 + 3X_2 \leq 6$ (Res1)
(Res 2 is completely variable)
New Opt output = (0,2) = 2
New Opt TPBFC = 68
New Opt TPAFC = 68-18 = 50
New Opt Res 2 = $2X_1 + 1X_2 = B_2$
  = 2 (0) + 1 (2) = 2
  = 2

Min TVC = $20X_1 + 10X_2$
Subject to $2X_1 + 3X_2 \leq 6$ (Res 1)
  $X_1 + X_2 = $ Output (param 0 to 10)
  (Res 2 completely variable)

IA

OA

(b) Returning to the original data (including the original product price) for the furniture firm in Problem 8.1, undertake an analysis of an increase in the Resource 2 (labor hour) cost from $11 to $14 Under this change, respond to the same questions raised in Problem 8.1 (a) through (i). Discuss the effect of the labor-cost change on the optimal output, the optimal output proram, and the optimal TPBFC and TPAFC.

9.2   (a) Changes for the automobile parts firm in Problem 8.2 are next to be studied. The product price has decreased from $48 to $36. Under this new product price, respond, using LINDO, to the questions asked in Problem 8.1 (a) through (i). Discuss the impact of the product-price decrease on the optimal output and the optimal TPBFC and TPAFC.

(b) Going back to all the original data in Problem 8.2 for this firm, undertake an analysis of an increase in the Resource 2 (labor hour) cost from $13 to $17. Under this increase answer the questions raised in Problem 8.1 (a) through (i). Discuss the effect of the labor-cost increase on the optimal output program, and the optimal TPBFC and TPAFC.

9.3   (a) Shoes are made by the firm in Problem 8.3. Now, a change in the product price has occurred, falling from $160 per unit to $144. Assuming all other data remain the same as in Problem 8.3, analyze the effect of this price decrease (using LINDO) by answering the questions raised in Problem 8.1 (a) through (i). Discuss the effect on the optimal output, the optimal output program, the optimal TPBFC and TPAFC.

(b) The effect of an increase in Resource 2 (labor hour) cost is now to be studied. It has increased from $19 to $22. Returning to all of the other data in Problem 8.3, analyze the effect of the questions raised in Problem 8.1 (a) through (i). Discuss the impact of the Resource 2 price increase on the optimal output, the optimal output program, and the optimal TPBFC and TPAFC.

9.4   (a) The firm making backpacks looks at a product-price increase from $64 to $96. With all other data remaining the same as in

Problem 8.4, study the effect by answering the questions raised in Problem 8.1 (a) through (i). Discuss the effect of the product-price increase on the optimal output, the optimal output program, and the optimal TPBFC and TPAFC.

(b) Let us do a separate analysis of a Resource 2 (labor hour) cost increase from $11 to $14. All other data from Problem 8.4 remain the same. Under the change in Resource 2 cost, answer the questions raised in Problem 8.1 (a) through (i). Discuss the effect on the optimal output, the optimal output program, and the optimal TPBFC and TPAFC.

10

Technological Change, Investment, and the Financial Industry

In this chapter, we examine the effects of an innovation in one of the processes involving a technological change and an increase in the productivity of both the machine input and the labor input.

We shall assume a change in Process 2, the mechanized process, that affects the rates of use of both resources in production by that process.

In our example, we represent the change in Diagram 10.1 where the mechanized Process 2 now requires, in producing a unit of output, only 2.4 machine hours (Resource 1) instead of 3, and requires only nine-tenths of a labor hour (Resource 2) rather than 1. The rest of the data table in Diagram 10.1 remains unchanged, including the product price of $48.

In doing the analysis shown in the earlier Diagram 9.1 under the original technology, we found that the increase in the product price to $48 (from $24) resulted in an increase in the optimal Resource 2 amount from 2 all the way to 6. This was accompanied by an increase in the optimal product output from 2 to 3 units. Now, we want to determine the effect of a technological change on the optimal amount of Resource 2 to acquire (and the optimal output to produce as well as how much by each process).

The results of doing this are shown in Diagram 10.1. Moreover, this is a good example to begin exploring the effects of various technological and productivity changes.

Even though it is an extremely simple case, we may be surprised at the results. Intuitively, we may not have foreseen that the technological change in Process 2 would cause the optimal Resource 2 input to fall from 6 to only 2¼ labor hours and the optimal product output to drop

Diagram 10.1 Technological Change in Process 2 With New Rates of Resource Use: Short-Run Analysis

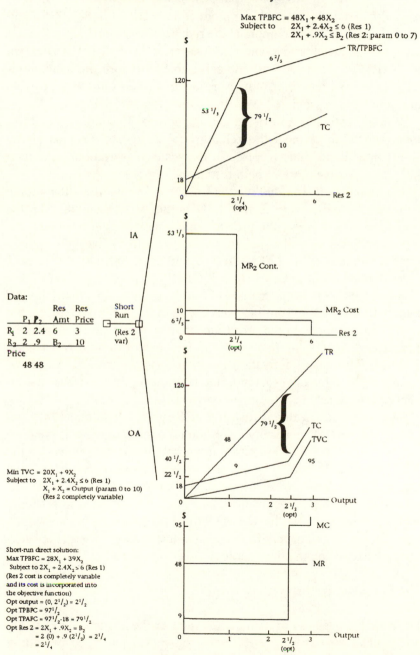

Max TPBFC = $48X_1 + 48X_2$
Subject to $\quad 2X_1 + 2.4X_2 \leq 6$ (Res 1)
$\qquad\qquad 2X_1 + .9X_2 \leq B_2$ (Res 2: param 0 to 7)

Data:

	Res	Res	
P_1 P_2	Amt	Price	
R_1 2 2.4	6	3	
R_2 2 .9	B_2	10	
Price			
48 48			

Short Run (Res 2 var)

Min TVC = $20X_1 + 9X_2$
Subject to $\quad 2X_1 + 2.4X_2 \leq 6$ (Res 1)
$\qquad\qquad X_1 + X_2 = $ Output (param 0 to 10)
$\qquad\qquad$ (Res 2 completely variable)

Short-run direct solution:
Max TPBFC = $28X_1 + 39X_2$
$\quad$ Subject to $2X_1 + 2.4X_2 \leq 6$ (Res 1)
(Res 2 cost is completely variable
and its cost is incorporated into
the objective function)
Opt output = $(0, 2^1/_2) = 2^1/_2$
Opt TPBPC = $97^1/_2$
Opt TPAFC = $97^1/_2 - 18 = 79^1/_2$
Opt Res 2 = $2X_1 + .9X_2 = B_2$
$\qquad = 2 (0) + .9 (2^1/_2) = 2^1/_4$
$\qquad = 2^1/_4$

from 3 units to 2½, even though the product price stays at $48.

Furthermore, all product output now is associated with the mechanized Process 2. Again, with the product price still at $48, TPBFC and TPAFC are both at a maximum at the reduced Resource 2 input amount (and at the reduced product output). As seen at the top right of Diagram 10.1, TPAFC is now $79.50 compared to $66 before the technological change. We have not, however, taken into account any possible additional cost associated with the technological change.

With the optimal profit rising and the optimal Resource 2 input (labor hours) falling owing to the technological change, the firm may, however, contemplate some increase in the scale of operations over time that might involve more of both resources.

The main results of *doubling* the Resource 1 input and allowing the Resource 2 input to vary is seen in Diagram 10.2. Assuming that the rates of resource usage (the productivities) remain constant under the new technology, as well as the product and resource prices, the optimal TPAFC doubles from $79.50 to $159 and the optimal Resource 2 input (labor hours) doubles from 2¼ to 4½.

When the technology change is accompanied by no greater investment in Resource 1, the optimal Resource 2 input falls from 6 to 2¼; but as the firm responds to the profit incentive it would find a substantial benefit from increasing investment in Resource 1 similar to what we assumed. Of course, motivation for even further expansion would be present if the rates of resource usage remained constant (thus, if constant returns to scale continued to prevail).

Such increases in the availability of Resource 1 amounts may not actually be possible generally under the leasing arrangements we have assumed and may instead require substantial investment outlays for the firm. This would typically be the case involving resources such as land and facilities as one moves toward more realistic examples. Moreover, internal accounting charges by the firm may actually result in costs similar to the leasing costs we have assumed for Resource 1. Naturally, the banking system and the entire financial industry play a big role in backing such expansion in all industries.

The Financial Industry

The primary business of some firms (and in the United States in the recent past, virtually their exclusive business) has been providing

Diagram 10.2   **Technological Change in Process 2 Combined With an Increase in the Scale of Operations**

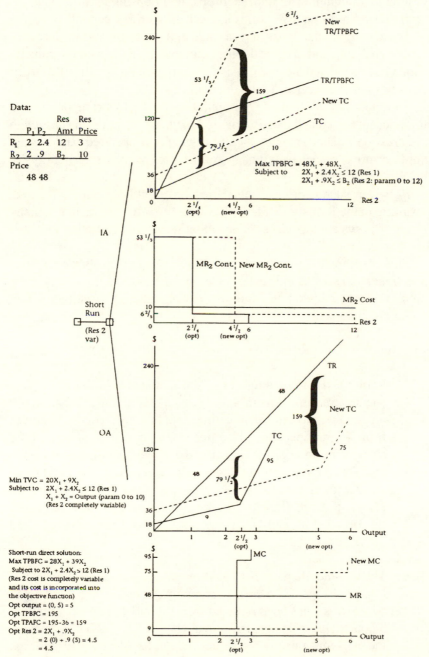

Data:

| | Res | Res |
P₁ P₂	Amt	Price
R₁ 2 2.4	12	3
R₂ 2 .9	B₂	10
Price		
48 48		

Max TPBFC = 48X₁ + 48X₂
Subject to   2X₁ + 2.4X₂ ≤ 12 (Res 1)
                    2X₁ + .9X₂ ≤ B₂ (Res 2: param 0 to 12)

IA

Short
Run

(Res 2
var)

OA

Min TVC = 20X₁ + 9X₂
Subject to   2X₁ + 2.4X₂ ≤ 12 (Res 1)
                   X₁ + X₂ = Output (param 0 to 10)
                   (Res 2 completely variable)

Short-run direct solution:
Max TPBFC = 28X₁ + 39X₂
   Subject to 2X₁ + 2.4X₂ ≤ 12 (Res 1)
(Res 2 cost is completely variable
and its cost is incorporated into
the objective function)
Opt output = (0, 5) = 5
Opt TPBFC = 195
Opt TPAFC = 195-36 = 159
Opt Res 2 = 2X₁ + .9X₂
          = 2 (0) + .9 (5) = 4.5
          = 4.5

funds to other firms and consumers to help finance long-term investments in equipment, land, facilities, and housing as well as short-term expenditures on inventories and other "working capital" needs.

These commercial banks and savings and loan associations have accepted checking and savings deposit accounts by firms and consumers, which have provided the main basis for such funding and the offering of various financial services to the depositors.

From its early years, the U.S. population has had a strong preference for a decentralized and locally oriented banking system. This has led to the creation of thousands of locally owned and operated banks. And, until recently, "branch banking" by out-of-state banks was generally not legal in most states.

However, such restrictive legislation has now been widely relaxed, resulting in the formation of large banking firms with branches in many states. The system today is similar to that found in many other industrialized nations.

This development has gone on as many firms in various manufacturing, trade, and service industries have become more national and international in their operations and are, perhaps, better served by larger commercial banks.

Problems

10.1   Return to the original furniture firm analyzed in Problem 8.1 (first encountered in Problem 4.1). Now, a technological change has resulted in the rate of machine hour use by Process 2 falling from 4 hours per unit of output to $3^1/_5$ hours. This is the only change from the original problem and we wish to know the effect. Therefore, after the technological change, use LINDO to answer the questions for this firm that were raised in Problem 8.1 (a) through (i). Discuss the impact on the optimal output, the optimal output program, and the optimal TPBFC and TPAFC.

10.2.   The automobile parts firm in Problem 8.2 has attained a technological change in Process 1. The rate of usage of machine hours by Process 1 has been reduced from 4 hours per unit of output to 3 hours. Under this technological change, use LINDO to answer the questions raised for another firm in Problem 8.1 (a) through

Box 10.1

Public Policies in the Financial Industry

Activities of the commercial banking industry affect virtually every other industry and consumer welfare as well. But experience has shown that while motivations based on self-interest work reasonably well in most other industries, the commercial banking industry is one in which there are periods when fluctuations in banking activities have become extreme and have had very adverse effects on virtually all other industries and consumers.

Thus, some federal government intervention in financial markets came to be viewed as generally desirable. This conclusion resulted in the formation of the Federal Reserve System in 1913.

Most of the commercial banks are members of the Federal Reserve System, which is headed by a federally appointed Board of Governors. This Federal Reserve Board is based in Washington, DC, but possesses some degree of independence from the federal government, being charged with formulating and implementing national monetary policy, especially short-term interest rates and the money supply. However, the chairman of the Board of Governors is required to report periodically to Congress on the board's policies and actions.

Thus, firms in all industries are affected by actions of the Federal Reserve Board in its attempts to promote orderly economic growth without inflation.

Much of the funding of long-term investments by firms in facilities, land, and equipment is undertaken by the sale of stocks and bonds in the financial markets through investment banks, most of which are located in New York's financial district (Wall Street). This provides a means of gaining access to a variety of sources for substantial funding. The federal Securities and Exchange Commission (SEC) plays a supervisory role in these markets.

(i). Discuss the impact on the optimal output, the optimal output program, and the optimal TPBFC and TPAFC.

10.3   The firm making shoes has encountered a decrease in the efficiency of labor due to a decrease in organizational effectiveness. This firm was encountered in Problem 8.3, and the effect of an increase in the rate of use of labor hours from 2 hours to 3 hours by Process 1 is to be studied. In order to compare the results with the original problem in Problem 8.3, use LINDO to answer the questions raised for another firm in Problem 8.1 (a) through (i). Discuss the impact of the change on the optimal output, the optimal output program, and the optimal TPBFC and TPAFC.

10.4   The backpack-making firm in Problem 8.4 has improved its organizational effectiveness and has decreased the rate of use of labor hours by Process 2 from 2 hours to 1 hour. Under this change, respond, using LINDO, to the questions asked for another firm in Problem 8.1 (a) through (i). Discuss the impact of the increased efficiency in labor on optimal output, the optimal output program, and the optimal TPBFC and TPAFC.

10.5   A firm makes football helmets and is confronted with the following data table showing the availabilities of two resources and their rates of usage by two processes.

	Process 1	Process 2	Resource amount available	Resource price
Resource 1 (machine hours)	4 hours	8 hours	24 hours	$6
Resource 2 (labor hours)	4 hours	2 hours	12 hours	$13
Product price	$84	$84		

(a) Using LINDO, respond for this firm to the questions raised for another firm in Problem 8.1 (a) through (i).

(b) This firm is considering a 25 percent increase in the amount of Resource 1 that would be accompanied by a decrease in the rate of machine hour usage from 8 hours to 6 hours per unit of output by Process 2. Using LINDO, respond to the new situation by answering for this firm the questions asked of another firm in Problem 8.1 (a) through (i). Discuss the impact on the optimal output, the optimal output program, and the optimal TPBFC and TPAFC (not taking into account the increased Resource 1 cost).

11

Departure From Competition in the Product Market

In some markets, competition breaks down, resulting in very few sellers or buyers, occasionally with only one seller or one buyer remaining. Thus, there exists in these markets some degree of monopoly power over the product price, or, in the case of resource markets, monopoly power over the resource price. It is common to refer to the single buyer in any market as a *monopsonist* and a single seller as a *monopolist*.

The Firm Becomes a Monopolist in the Product Market

In our continuing exposition we undertake another transition for our firm where it becomes a single seller in the product market, thus, a monopolist.

If we go back to the competitive situation in Diagram 9.1 with a product price of $48 (along with the original technology) and then have the monopoly develop, we can, in the short-run analysis, trace its effect on the firm's optimal amount of output by each process, the optimal Resource 2 amount, and the optimal TPBFC.

In Diagram 9.1 we found the optimal output to be 3 units, all produced by the labor-intensive Process 1. Optimal TPAFC was $66 and the optimal Resource 2 amount was 6.

As seen in the data table in Diagram 11.1, we start the analysis with the Resource 2 amount at 6 and all elements, except the product price, corresponding to those in Diagram 9.1.

In the case of monopolistic firms, the price obtained for the product output depends upon the amount placed on the market. In Diagram 11.1

we have a very simple example showing the product price of $48 when 3 units are produced, increasing to a price of $60 for 2 units, and $72 if only 1 unit is produced.

We go ahead and construct a table from our short-run parameterization of output. Total variable cost is minimized subject to the Resource 1 constraint and a product output constraint as seen in the output analysis section of Diagram 11.1. Resource 2 is completely variable, with its cost captured in the objective function.

The graphical depictions and the output analysis table clearly show that the optimal output is 2 units (with TPAFC of $82) for the monopolistic firm compared to 3 units (and TPAFC of $66) when it was still a single firm in a competitive market. With output at 2 units, a price of $60 can be obtained rather then $48. This is clearly a blow to the buyers.

But what about the optimal amount to hire of Resource 2 (labor hours)? Having done the output analysis first, we have already obtained the optimal output program, which we can insert into our Resource 2 equation representing its usage for various programs. Here, we see the optimal Resource 2 amount to be 2. And this is a big decline from the optimal Resource 2 amount of 6 when the firm was competitive.

Reviewing the result of the firm becoming a monopolist, we see that the product output is reduced from 3 to 2 units to the detriment of buyers, and Resource 2 employment is reduced from 6 to 2, resulting in substantial downsizing of Resource 2.

The optimal output program shifts from (3,0) to (0,2), revealing a shift from the entire output (3 units) by the labor-intensive Process 1 to all of the output (2 units) being produced by the mechanized Process 2.

Two Sellers in the Product Market: A Game Model

If the number of sellers in a market is two, a special type of situation emerges that has been characterized as essentially equivalent to a game between the two rivals.

If the two firms were to collude and agree on output (and thus on price), their combined action could approach the situation of the monopolist in Diagram 11.1. But if the firms acted independently, uncertainty could exist regarding the rival firm's output and, therefore, the price that could be obtained.

Our short-run analysis of this type of situation appears in Diagram 11.2. The data table is assumed to be the same for both Firm A and Firm B,

Diagram 11.1 **Monopoly in the Product Market**

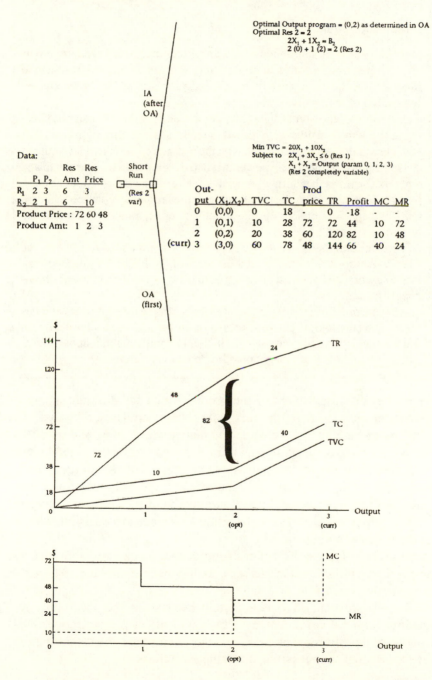

Optimal Output program = (0,2) as determined in OA
Optimal Res 2 = 2
$$2X_1 + 1X_2 = B_2$$
$$2(0) + 1(2) = 2 \text{ (Res 2)}$$

IA
(after
OA)

Data:

	Res	Res
$P_1\,P_2$	Amt	Price
R_1 2 3	6	3
R_2 2 1	6	10

Product Price : 72 60 48
Product Amt: 1 2 3

Short
Run

(Res 2
var)

Min TVC = $20X_1 + 10X_2$
Subject to $2X_1 + 3X_2 \leq 6$ (Res 1)
 $X_1 + X_2 = $ Output (param 0, 1, 2, 3)
 (Res 2 completely variable)

Out-put	(X_1,X_2)	TVC	TC	Prod price	TR	Profit	MC	MR
0	(0,0)	0	18	-	0	-18	-	-
1	(0,1)	10	28	72	72	44	10	72
2	(0,2)	20	38	60	120	82	10	48
(curr) 3	(3,0)	60	78	48	144	66	40	24

OA
(first)

Box 11.1

Antimonopoly Policies

In the early years of the United States, an agricultural-based economy, combined with a very favorable cultural setting, allowed a free market system to flourish. But the emergence of canals and railroads in the 1800s created some areas of monopoly power.

In 1886 the federal Interstate Commerce Commission was established to regulate pricing and other activities of the railroads. Another significant federal intervention occurred in 1890 with the passage of the Sherman Antitrust Act in response to monopoly power that had developed in the petroleum and other industries as they formed special "trust" arrangements to reduce competition. The most prominent application of the law occurred when Standard Oil Company was broken up into a number of separate units in order to restore competition.

Further controls on anticompetitive activity were added in 1914 by the Clayton Antitrust Act and the establishment of the Federal Trade Commission to enforce the antitrust laws and help prevent the development of monopoly power.

The dynamics of markets in the late 1900s, driven by significant and far-reaching technological changes, created a movement of federal policy toward deregulation and even some hesitation in combating monopoly power, which in some cases is thought possibly to be only temporary.

---

including their assessment of the product price for different amounts placed on the market by the firms taken together. Thus, $48 could be obtained by each firm if the combined output was 2 units; $36 would be the price for a total output of 3 and $24, for a combined output of 4 units.

A tree diagram of the short-run analysis (with Resource 2 variable) appears in Diagram 11.2. The tree analysis focuses on the situation of Firm A; however, Firm B faces an identical decision problem.

The output analysis (OA) in Diagram 11.2 leads to a decision point (a square) where output can be chosen to be 1 or 2 units (middle of Diagram 11.2). Total cost (TC) of each output amount can be determined by using linear programming analysis, as has been done here: $28 for 1 unit of output and $38 for 2 units.

But total revenue (TR) is uncertain because of the uncertainty regarding the rival firm's output, which will affect product price. This causes total profit for each firm to be uncertain; thus, the determination of the optimal output is not the same as before.

Diagram 11.2   Game Model of a Firm With One Rival That Has Identical Technology and Costs (Resource 2 input for each firm is variable)

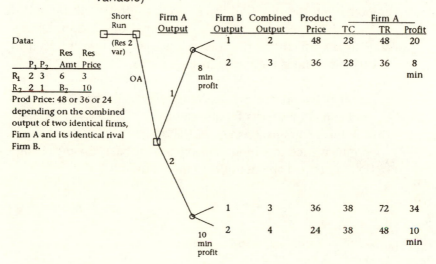

	Firm A Output	Firm B Output	Combined Output	Product Price	TC	Firm A TR	Profit
		1	2	48	28	48	20
		2	3	36	28	36	8 min
		1	3	36	38	72	34
		2	4	24	38	48	10 min

Data:

	Res	Res	(Res 2 var)
	P_1	P_2	Amt Price
R_1	2	3	6 3
R_2	2	1	B_2 10

Prod Price: 48 or 36 or 24 depending on the combined output of two identical firms, Firm A and its identical rival Firm B.

By the maximin (pessimist) criterion the best output for Firm A (and for the identical Firm B) is 2 units, which has the highest minimum profit of $10. This is a stable (equilibrium) solution since there is no incentive for either firm to change its output given that each firm uses the maximin criterion.

Collusion could result by each firm agreeing to restrict output to 1 unit each, doubling the profit to each from $10 to $20.

Perhaps the most defensible decision criterion to use in such situations is the "maximin" criterion, also known as the "pessimist" criterion. The term is a contraction of the phrase "maximization of minimum outcomes." The corollary in cost problems is the "minimax" criterion.

The procedure for selecting the best output by this criterion is quite straightforward. We lay out all of the combinations of Firm A's outputs and those of Firm B, along with the total profit consequences. We then identify the minimum total profit that can occur for each output choice and from this set of minimum outcomes select the maximum.

Thus, the solution using this criterion is for Firm A (and also Firm B) to produce 2 units and thus be assured of $10 of total profit.

Problems

11.1   The automobile-parts firm in Problems 5.2 has now found itself in a monopoly-type situation where buyers of its product output have no close substitutes. The firm can now obtain a higher price per unit of output as it reduces output. The output amounts and the resulting prices are as follows: an output of 3, $48; an output of 6, $42; and an output of 12, $36. Undertake an analysis of the firm (as in Diagram 11.1 with Resource 2 variable) under the changed conditions.

(a) Identify the optimal product output under the new conditions and explain the basis for any change.
(b) Obtain the optimal Resource 2 (labor) input under the changed product-price conditions and explain the basis for any change in the optimal amount of Resource 2 to hire.

12

Departure From Competition in the Labor Market

Let us consider the transition of our example firm into a monopsonist in the Resource 2 (labor) market. In this case, our firm has become the sole buyer of labor in the Resource 2 market and consequently has substantial influence over the resource price (here, of course, the price is the wage rate).

To trace the effects of this change, we leave all of the data of the firm unchanged from those in Diagram 9.1 except for the price of Resource 2.

The price of Resource 2 to the firm, however, is now affected by the amount of Resource 2 purchased. This price information is included in Diagram 12.1 along with other data.

As seen in the data table of Diagram 12.1, when the firm acquires more of Resource 2 its price is driven upward and, conversely, if less is sought the price to be paid is lowered.

We start the analysis in Diagram 12.1 with the Resource 2 amount at 6 with a price of $10, a product price of $48, and the original technology. On the graphs for the short-run analysis, we repeat that optimal Resource 2 amount of 6 that we found under those conditions shown in Diagram 9.1.

But now when the firm affects the Resource 2 price by its actions, our short-run analysis gets more complicated. To keep it simple, we have resorted to limited use of tables as we parameterize Resource 2 to obtain graphically the new optimal Resource 2 amount of 4. This we show in Diagram 12.1.

The optimal output amount of 2½ units (and the optimal program revealing the optimal combination of processes) can then be determined by using the optimal Resource 2 amount of 4 obtained in the input analysis

Diagram 12.1   **Monopsony in the Resource 2 Market**

Max TPBFC = $48X_1 + 48X_2$
Subject to $\quad 2X_1 + 3X_2 \le 6$ (Res 1)
$\qquad\qquad 2X_1 + 1X_2 \le B_2$ (Res 2: param 0 to 7)

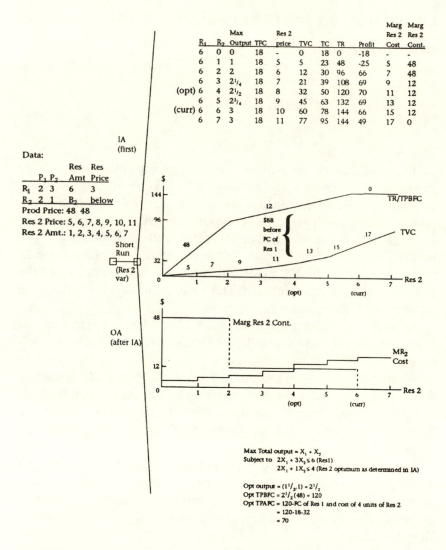

R_1	R_2	Max Output	TFC	Res 2 price	TVC	TC	TR	Profit	Marg Res 2 Cost	Marg Res 2 Cont.
6	0	0	18	-	0	18	0	-18	-	-
6	1	1	18	5	5	23	48	-25	5	48
6	2	2	18	6	12	30	96	66	7	48
6	3	$2^1/_4$	18	7	21	39	108	69	9	12
(opt) 6	4	$2^1/_2$	18	8	32	50	120	70	11	12
6	5	$2^3/_4$	18	9	45	63	132	69	13	12
(curr) 6	6	3	18	10	60	78	144	66	15	12
6	7	3	18	11	77	95	144	49	17	0

Data:

	Res	Res	
$P_1\ P_2$	Amt	Price	
R_1 2 3	6	3	
R_2 2 1	B_2	below	

Prod Price: 48 48
Res 2 Price: 5, 6, 7, 8, 9, 10, 11
Res 2 Amt.: 1, 2, 3, 4, 5, 6, 7

Short
Run
(Res 2
var)

IA
(first)

OA
(after IA)

Max Total output = $X_1 + X_2$
Subject to $2X_1 + 3X_2 \le 6$ (Res1)
$\qquad 2X_1 + 1X_2 \le 4$ (Res 2 optimum as determined in IA)

Opt output = $(1^1/_2, 1) = 2^1/_2$
Opt TPBFC = $2^1/_2(48) = 120$
Opt TPAFC = 120-PC of Res 1 and cost of 4 units of Res 2
$\qquad = 120-18-32$
$\qquad = 70$

(IA). We get the optimal output by creating and solving the linear programming formulation in the output analysis (OA) section in the lower part of Diagram 12.1.

The interesting results of the analysis are these: (1) As a monopsonist in the Resource 2 market, the firm finds the optimal Resource 2 amount falls from 6 to 4, paying $8 per unit of Resource 2 instead of the former $10; and (2) the optimal amount of product output, the price of which remained at $48, falls from 3 (as seen earlier in Diagram 9.1) to 2½. All in all, we see the wage rate falling from $10 to $8 with less employment and product availability also declining.

Now, the (1½, 1) optimal output program reveals a shift from the premonopsonist optimal program of (3,0) where all 3 units were produced by the labor-intensive Process 1. Now only 1½ units are produced by that process and 1 unit (instead of none) is produced by the mechanized Process 2.

We see again that we would be hard-pressed to arrive at these optimal values by intuitive or modest arithmetic procedures.

Labor Unions

The organization of employees into labor unions also provides an illustration of the development of monopoly power on the part of sellers—in this case, workers in the labor market. However, legislation in most developed countries has actually encouraged attainment of this monopoly power through unionization, in part, at least, because of the growth of monopsony power on the part of employers in the labor market, and also to some extent because of the perceived presence of monopoly power in the employers' product markets.

"Craft" unions, those associated with special skill areas such as carpentry and bricklaying, had a presence in the United States in the 1800s in some regions and encompassed concerns for productivity and performance as well as some means of control over a type of labor supply.

Such labor unions have a degree of monopoly influence on specific wage rates, especially in "closed shop" arrangements where employers are forced to hire only workers who are already union members.

It was in the 1930s that labor unions in the United States began to organize widely along industry lines. This increased greatly their role in wage determination and work issues in major industries such as automobile manufacturing, steel-making, and the like.

This development was greatly encouraged by federal legislation that was enacted in the 1930s giving effective protection to workers in their attempts at self-organization. Thus, wage determination and other work

---

Box 12.1

Labor Legislation

The main labor law enacted in the 1930s, whose coverage was extended to most industries, was the National Labor Relations Act of 1935. Also known as the Wagner Act after its sponsor, its main provisions are the following:

1. Various "unfair labor practices" by firms were specified:

    (a) interference with employees' attempts to form a union;
    (b) discrimination against any union employee because of union activities;
    (c) failure to bargain in good faith (with a union elected by employees) and to incorporate the results into a written contract.

2. The National Labor Relations Board (NLRB) was established to carry out the provisions of the National Labor Relations Act. The board performs the role of holding elections for employees to determine whether a majority wishes to have a specific union represent them in bargaining with their employer.

3. The NLRB was also given powers to investigate claims of unfair labor practices by firms.

In 1947, Congress passed the Taft-Hartley Act, which, among other things, outlined "unfair labor practices" with which labor unions could be charged and included a provision allowing the President of the United States to intervene in any strike that had widespread adverse effects upon the national welfare. The President's action can delay the strike for 30 days during which time the Federal Mediation and Conciliation Service attempts to resolve the dispute.

---

issues in many industries have become influenced by the relative bargaining power between employers and labor unions.

Problems

12.1 Suppose the shoe-making firm in Problem 5.3 became a monopsonist, the single buyer of Resource 2 (labor). Thus, the price of

Resource 2 (labor) is affected by the amount hired. Now, it sees the current cost of $19 per hour falling as the amount hired is reduced: 7 hours, $18; 6 hours, $17; 5 hours, $16; 4 hours or less, $15.

Undertake an analysis of the firm (as in Diagram 12.1) under these changed conditions, with Resource 2 a variable input as before.

(a) What is the optimal output under the new conditions? Explain the basis for any change.
(b) Identify the optimal Resource 2 input under the new conditions and explain the basis for any change.

13

Uncertainty in Product Price: Risk Neutrality and Risk Aversion

Except for the game-type situation illustrated earlier in Diagram 11.2, we have not confronted the common problem of firms being faced with uncertainty in product prices or uncertainty regarding some other important elements in their situations.

All other examples that we have encountered so far depicted instances where an optimal program of output or an optimal resource input could be determined and the profit consequence could be known in advance. Thus, such models of situations are referred to as "deterministic" or "certainty" models.

It is important to note that in such models the certainty is *assumed* to exist even though the user of the model (here, the firm) may be uncertain about the product price or some other parameter value that was assumed in the model.

At times, therefore, a more useful model to deal with uncertainty when it exists, such as in product price, may be one that attempts to assess the *degree* of uncertainty by assigning *probabilities* to the different price possibilities. We discuss this approach and provide a simple illustration in Diagram 13.1. [*Note:* Decision analysis under uncertainty (with different risk preferences and the revision of initial probabilities after the receipt of additional information) is discussed in my *Statistics for Decisions* (Little, Brown, 1972).]

To keep it simple, we continue with our familiar firm, introducing uncertainty in the product price and focusing on an analysis of the short-run period where Resource 2 can be varied. First, we vary Resource 2 parametrically, as before, so as to generate the useful graphical analysis;

Diagram 13.1 **Product-Price Uncertainty and a Risk-Neutral Firm**

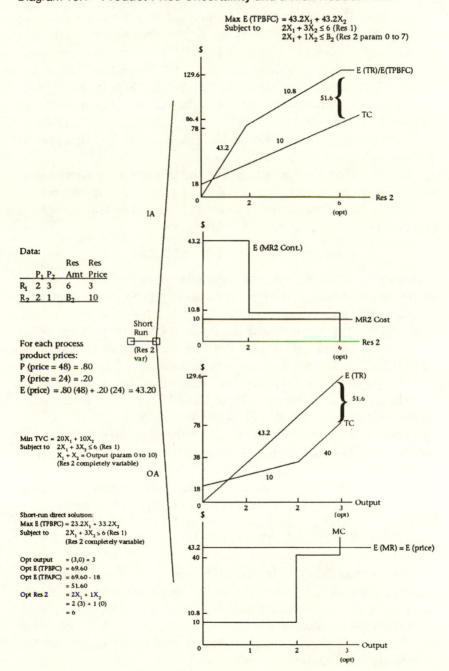

Max E (TPBFC) $= 43.2X_1 + 43.2X_2$
Subject to $\quad 2X_1 + 3X_2 \le 6$ (Res 1)
$\quad\quad\quad 2X_1 + 1X_2 \le B_2$ (Res 2 param 0 to 7)

IA

Data:

		Res	Res
	$P_1\ P_2$	Amt	Price
R_1	2 3	6	3
R_2	2 1	B_2	10

Short
Run
(Res 2
var)

For each process
product prices:
P (price $= 48$) $= .80$
P (price $= 24$) $= .20$
E (price) $= .80 (48) + .20 (24) = 43.20$

Min TVC $= 20X_1 + 10X_2$
Subject to $\quad 2X_1 + 3X_2 \le 6$ (Res 1)
$\quad\quad\quad X_1 + X_2 =$ Output (param 0 to 10)
$\quad\quad\quad$ (Res 2 completely variable)

OA

Short-run direct solution:
Max E (TPBFC) $= 23.2X_1 + 33.2X_2$
Subject to $\quad 2X_1 + 3X_2 \le 6$ (Res 1)
$\quad\quad\quad$ (Res 2 completely variable)

Opt output $\quad = (3,0) = 3$
Opt E (TPBFC) $= 69.60$
Opt E (TPAFC) $= 69.60 - 18$
$\quad\quad\quad\quad = 51.60$
Opt Res 2 $\quad = 2X_1 + 1X_2$
$\quad\quad\quad\quad = 2 (3) + 1 (0)$
$\quad\quad\quad\quad = 6$

later, we shift to the direct-solution approach in reaching the same optimal Resource 2 amount and the same optimal program of output.

Thus, the degree of uncertainty regarding product price possibilities is assessed and probabilities are assigned to the various price possibilities.

As seen in the data table of Diagram 13.1, our simple version assumes only two product price possibilities, $48 and $24. Based on existing knowledge, perhaps derived from relative frequency data and an intuitive understanding of the market forces, a probability of .80 is assigned to the occurrence of a $48 price and a probability of .20 is assigned to the occurrence of a $24 price.

Then, with probabilities attached to the product-price possibilities, we can, before any analysis is undertaken, compute the "expected price," in short, E (price). As shown in Diagram 13.1 and below, we see the expected product price is $43.20.

$$E \text{ (price)} = .80 \ (\$48) + .20 \ (\$24) = \$43.20.$$

A common interpretation of an expected price is that it can be thought of as a future average price based on the set of probabilities assumed for different price possibilities.

It employs the notion that if the future relative frequencies of the prices are in accord with the probabilities assumed, an average price equal to the "expected price" would be realized.

Thus, we now have an expected price for the output by each process and can use its value, here $43.20, in place of the earlier certain price amounts (and unit revenues) of $24 and, later, $48.

As before, in some situations we can use the expected price (expected unit revenue) as the coefficients in the objective function for output by each process.

This, however, will give us an "expected total revenue" E (TR) or "expected total profit before fixed cost" E (TPBFC) for each program. Of course, generally, we seek the maximum E (TPBFC), which at times is equal to the maximum E (TR). And, subtracting the fixed cost from E (TPBFC) gives us E (TPAFC).

In the input analysis (IA) section of Diagram 13.1, we parameterize the Resource 2 amount and generate the familiar graphical analysis that clearly indicates the optimal Resource 2 amount is 6, with an E (TPAFC) of $51.60.

In the output analysis (OA) section of Diagram 13.1 we minimize total variable cost (TVC) and parameterize total output to generate the desired graphical analysis.

The product-price uncertainty in the output analysis comes in through the E (TR) graph with a slope of $43.20, equal to the E (price). We see the optimal product output is 3 units with the same E (TPAFC) of $51.60. Although it is not shown, we can compute the optimal output program, which is (3,0), all output being done by the labor-intensive Process 1.

But the analysis in Diagram 13.1 is appropriate only in some situations. There has to be evidence that the firm is *risk neutral*. This means that each dollar of profit that may be gained or lost is of equal importance. If this is true, the analysis in Diagram 13.1 is valid.

But if dollars of profit that might be gained or lost are not equal in importance, some modification in the objective function will have to be made to reflect the greater importance of some dollars of profit compared to others.

A common "risk preference" pattern for profit amounts is that called "risk aversion" where, going from the lowest profit outcome to the highest, each additional dollar of profit has less and less importance. Thus, a concave graph of this relationship would be appropriate, such as the one shown in the lower section of Diagram 13.2. The common name for such a measure of the strength of preference of various amounts of some objective, such as profit, is a *utility function*. It would be unique to a firm or individual.

From the utility-for-profit graph we can "read off" a utility value for each profit amount as is done in the middle of Diagram 13.2 in the tree analysis developed to select the optimal product amount for our risk-averse firm.

Above each circled chance point in the main decision tree we record the computed expected profit. But we have noted that its maximization is not an appropriate criterion for a risk-averse firm. However, we do see again that the output of 3 units does maximize expected total profit at $51.60, as shown earlier in Diagram 13.1.

But for our risk-averse firm we need to maximize expected utility, which may be associated with an output that is not the one that maximizes expected total profit.

In the tree analysis in Diagram 13.2 we obtain an expected utility for each output by multiplying possible utility outcomes of each output by the associated probabilities and summing the products. Thus, for an output of 2 units we have an expected utility of .9380, which actually is the output with the maximum expected utility:

Diagram 13.2   **Product-Price Uncertainty and a Risk-Averse Firm**
(now, utility for profit values are needed and are derived)

Data:

		Res	Res		Out-			If Product price is $48		If Product price is $24	
	P_1 P_2	Amt	Price		put	(X_1,X_2)	TC	TR	Profit	TR	Profit
R_1	2 3	6	3		0	(0,0)	18	0	-18	0	-18
R_2	2 1	B_2	10		1	(0,1)	28	48	20	24	-4

Product prices: — Short
P (price = 48) = .80   — Run
P (price = 24) = .20

2	(0,2)	38	96	58	48	10
3	(3,0)	78	144	66	72	-6

Opt output: 2; E(U) = .9380
Opt Res 2: $2X_1 + 1X_2 =$
             $= 2(0) + 1(2) = 2$

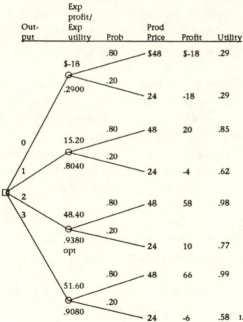

Out-put	Exp profit/ Exp utility	Prob	Prod Price	Profit	Utility
	$-18 .2900	.80	$48	$-18	.29
		.20	24	-18	.29
0 1	15.20 .8040	.80	48	20	.85
		.20	24	-4	.62
2 3	48.40 .9380 opt	.80	48	58	.98
		.20	24	10	.77
	51.60 .9080	.80	48	66	.99
		.20	24	-6	.58

Derivation of utility for profit of $0:
Probabilities varied until equal preference

	equal preference	Profit	Utility
	.66	$80	1.00
E(U) = .66 Act 1			
Act 2	.34	-20	.00
E(U) = .66		0	(.66)

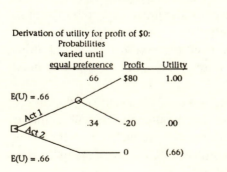

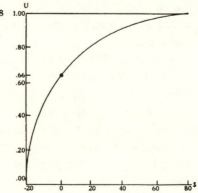

$$E\ (U) = .80\ (.98) + .20\ (.77) = .9380.$$

From the utility graph the utility was found to be approximately .98 for a profit of $58 and for a profit of $10 the utility is close to .77.

But how did we obtain the specific concave utility graph for our firm? First of all, we need to identify the range of profit outcomes that is relevant. Here a range from –$20 to $80 is sufficient because all profit possibilities fall within that range. And, as is common, we place the profit values on the horizontal axis of the graph.

We need to develop utility values for profit amounts in this range; thus, a first step would be to assign a utility of .00 to the lowest profit of –$20, and a utility of 1.00 to the highest profit of $80. This immediately gives us two points on the utility graph.

In an actual situation we would like to obtain more than one additional utility value for profit amounts between –$20 and $80, but obtaining the utility for just one profit amount will illustrate the procedure.

Choosing a profit amount toward the lower end of the profit possibilities will usually be quite revealing regarding the degree of the concavity of the utility graph and thus the degree of risk aversion. Therefore, we chose a profit amount of $0 to illustrate the modern procedure for deriving a utility value for this profit amount.

The procedure is this: On the side create a *separate* decision tree, one that has but two "act-branches" emanating from a decision point. We do this in the lower section of Diagram 13.2. One act-branch, Act 2, will have a certain profit outcome of $0 (which we selected); the other act-branch, Act 1, will have two profit possibilities. One possibility will be the highest profit in our assumed range of profit possibilities (here $80); the other possibility will be the lowest (here –$20).

We begin by temporarily assigning probabilities to the two extreme outcomes of Act 1, and then vary the probabilities until equal preference for the two acts is indicated by the subject (the firm).

A typical way to start would be to assign a probability of 1.00 to the $80 profit outcome and .00 to the –$20 profit outcome. This first probability assignment may seem trivial but it gets the procedure under way to obtain ultimately a crucial utility value for the total profit of $0.

Of course, in the first round of probability assignments we would typically foresee a clear preference for Act 1, which, with this set of probability assignments, would have a sure profit of $80 compared to a certain $0 for Act 2.

But as we decrease the probability of the $80 outcome from 1.00 and increase the probability of the −$20 outcome of Act 1, serious thought should start to set in regarding the preferred act. (Remember that the probabilities must sum to 1.00.)

Once *equal preference* for the two acts is indicated, we have valuable information. We assume in this example that equal preference is shown when the probabilities are .66 on the $80 and .34 on −$20.

But how does this result give us information on the utility value for a profit of $0? By taking another step. As indicated before, we are assigning a utility of 1.00 to the highest profit possibility of $80 and a utility of .00 to the lowest, which is −$20.

Thus, attaching these utilities to the extremes profit possibilities of Act 1 we can compute the expected utility of Act 1 with the designated probabilities of .66 for a utility of 1.00 and .34 for a utility of .00:

$$\text{Expected utility of Act 1 at the point of equal preference} = .66\,(1.00) + .34\,(.00) = .66.$$

The final step is this: Because equal preference for the two acts has been shown, the expected utility of the two acts should be the same. And, because we have obtained the expected utility of Act 1, which is .66, we can assert that the expected utility of Act 2 should be the same.

But as there is only one profit outcome of Act 2 (the outcome implicitly having a probability of 1.00), the expected utility of .66 for Act 2 implies a utility of .66 for the one profit outcome of $0.

On our utility graph at the bottom of Diagram 13.2 we record the utility value of .66 for a profit of $0. Then, with a utility of .00 for −$20 and a utility of 1.00 for $80, we have three points, which, when fit by using a French curve, gives us the utility graph that we used to obtain all of the utility values for profit in the main decision tree.

The Possibility of Additional Information

In circumstances involving uncertainty regarding some important element in a decision, it is common to contemplate the possible reduction of the uncertainty before the decision is made. And, in our context, additional information about such things as future product prices is often possible to obtain. But an important question surrounds the value of the additional information and its relation to its cost. Because additional information is often imperfect as a predictor, it is not uncommon for its cost to exceed its expected value to the decision maker.

In Diagram 13.3 we portray a simplified case involving our familiar firm contemplating obtaining additional information regarding the future product price (essentially, the "state" of the market) before an output decision is made. [*Note:* Decision-tree software programs, such as Arborist from Texas Instruments, are available for the larger, practical decision-under-uncertainty problems.]

This case is an extension of the firm's situation in Diagram 13.2 where current uncertainty regarding product price was incorporated into the decision on product output. Because we assumed risk aversion in the firm, we needed to attach the firm's appropriate utility values to the profit outcomes and compute an expected utility for each output action in order to obtain the optimal decision.

In the upper portion of Diagram 13.3 we repeat the tree analysis of Diagram 13.2, which focused on current information about the product price. Here we recognize that the probabilities assigned to the profit and utility outcomes represent current information or information prior to the possible attainment of additional information. Thus, the term "prior probabilities" is an appropriate description of such probabilities. And, under the prior-information section of the tree in Diagram 13.3 we see the same expected profit and expected utility analysis that was undertaken in Diagram 13.2.

Again, we see that under prior information the optimal output for our risk-averse firm is 2 units with the maximum expected utility of .9380, whereas the output with the maximum expected profit of $51.60 is 3 units. And, as we noted before, an output of 3 units would be optimal for a risk-neutral firm since the maximization of expected profit would be a valid decision criterion for such a firm.

Thus, if a firm shows clear evidence of being risk neutral, there would be no need to derive a utility graph for it. Even if one did derive a utility graph for such a firm, it would be a straight-line graph, and expected utility computations based on it would yield the same optimal action as that obtained by maximizing expected profit.

The lower section of the main decision tree in Diagram 13.3 shows, perhaps as simply as possible, the type of analysis necessary to obtain an indication of whether a given bit of information is worthwhile.

To do this, we need to obtain a revised set of price probabilities (of the "states") after a "reading" from some imperfect predictor has been

Diagram 13.3 **Product-Price Uncertainty With the Option of Obtaining Additional Information Before the Decision**

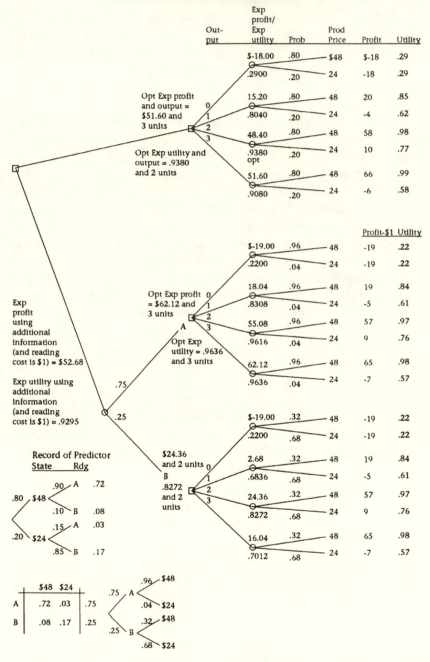

obtained. In our example, two possible readings can be obtained, Reading A and Reading B. And two price-possibility "states" are assumed, a product price of $48 and $24.

A glance at the main decision tree in Diagram 13.3 shows at the extreme left a decision point confronting the firm on whether actually to proceed on the upper prior-information branch, or to take the lower branch, which entails waiting to make the output decision until a reading has been obtained from the predictor. Our procedure will provide a rational basis for making that choice, which the firm faces at the extreme left decision point.

In the prior-information section of the main decision tree in Diagram 13.3, we have already found the optimal output and its expected utility for the risk-averse firm as well as the optimal expected profit for the risk-neutral firm. Now, however, we move these results backward (to the left) so they can be compared with our computations of the expected utility and expected profit using the additional information optimally; that is, by actually waiting to make the output decision until a reading has been received from the predictor and after appropriate revisions in the probabilities of the price-possibilities have been made.

Essentially, we want to do the same analysis after each reading as we did under the prior-information situation. But the revised ("posterior") probabilities will be different after each possible reading. Therefore, we need to repeat the output-decision analysis after each reading, which enlarges the tree considerably. (We shall discuss later the computation of the posterior probabilities.)

Also, the cost of the additional information (a reading) needs to be subtracted from the profit outcomes at the tips of the branches in the lower section of the main decision tree. We assume each reading incurs a cost of $1.00. Thus, in the analysis of the use of the additional information both the profit outcomes and the utility outcomes of the output actions are altered.

Looking at the posterior probabilities that we have inserted in the main decision tree after Reading A, we see them to have been revised upward from .80 on the price of $48 (under prior information only) to .96 after the receipt of Reading A. And the prior probability of the price of $24 has been revised downward from .20 to .04.

After Reading A, the expected utility analysis for our risk-averse firm identifies an output of 3 units as optimal with an expected utility of .9636. This represents an output increase from the optimal output of 2 units under prior information alone. We move this optimal expected utility and the associated optimal output of 3 backward (to the left) near Reading A.

After Reading A, the risk-neutral firm finds the maximum expected profit of $62.12 would be attained with an output of 3 units as well (middle of Diagram 13.3). This is the same optimal output identified under prior information alone for the risk-neutral firm. We move this output and its expected profit backward, too, and associate this with the risk-neutral firm.

Repeating the same analysis after Reading B gives us quite different posterior probabilities on the price possibilities compared to those after Reading A. Now, the probability of $48 is revised downward from .80 to .32 and the probability of the lower price of $24 is revised upward from .20 to .68. The computation of new expected utilities and expected profits is necessary. Now, both the risk-averse firm and the risk-neutral firm find the same output of 2 units to be optimal. The maximum expected utility is at an output of 2 for the risk-averse firm. It is .8272. And the maximum expected profit is at the same output of 2 for the risk-neutral firm. It is $24.36. As before, we move both of these expected value measures backward (to the left) near Reading B.

But before the decision can be made as to whether the additional information should be obtained, we have to position ourselves again at the decision point at the extreme left in Diagram 13.3. What is desired at that decision point is an expected value measure of the two alternatives: one for making the decision under prior information only, as in the upper section of the main decision tree; the other, for waiting on a reading from the predictor and then making the optimal output decision after the reading. We have identified the best act and its optimal expected value under prior information for each of the two firms and have moved each to the decision point at the left side of the main decision tree. We need, as well, an expected value measure for each firm going down the branch that represents obtaining a reading before making the output decision. To do this we focus again on the lower section of the main decision tree at points just posterior to each reading. At those points our conditional analysis reveals the best expected utility and best expected profit relevant to our firms after each reading.

What we need now is an expected utility and an expected profit *before* we know which reading will occur. And from our later probability analysis we shall learn how to compute the probability of each reading from its record and the prior information (which we are assuming is the same for each firm).

For now, however, let us simply place the probability of Reading A on the branch leading to Reading A. And we do the same for Reading B. It is .75 on Reading A and .25 on Reading B. Therefore, the probability of Reading A, which is .75, gives a probability of .75 on reaching the point where the risk-averse firm faces an optimal expected utility of .9636 (which we identified previously for the risk-averse firm after Reading A). With the probability of .25 on receiving Reading B, the risk-averse firm would then face an optimal expected utility of .8272.

Now, backing up to the decision point at the extreme left of Diagram 13.3 we see the need for an expected value going down the branch and using additional information when it is not known in advance which reading will be provided. But we have computed the probability of each reading.

This final expected value computation involves multiplying the probability of Reading A (which is .75) by the best expected value conditional on the receipt of that reading and then multiplying the probability of Reading B (which is .25) by the best expected value given that reading, after which we sum the two products to get the expected value using the additional information.

The computation for the risk-averse firm is as follows:

Expected utility using additional information = .75 (.9636) + .25 (.8272) = .9295.

We record this expected utility on the branch leading to the use of additional information by that firm.

For the risk-neutral firm, the expected profit using additional information would be obtained by the following computation:

Expected profit using additional information = .75 ($62.12) + .25 ($24.36) = $52.68.

The final step is to compare, for each firm, the expected result derived from making the output decision under prior information alone with the expected result derived by using the additional information as represented in our analysis.

As shown in Diagram 13.3, the findings are quite interesting. It turns out that the risk-neutral firm's expected profit using additional information (and taking into account its cost) is greater than that if the output decision was made under prior information alone: $52.68 vs. $51.60. Because we have taken into account its cost, the expected value of the additional information after its cost is $1.08: ($52.68 − $51.60).

For the risk-averse firm in this instance, the expected utility using additional information (and taking into account its cost) is lower than the expected utility under prior information alone. The optimal expected utility under prior information is .9380, whereas the expected utility using additional information is .9295. Thus, the analysis does not justify obtaining additional information by the risk-averse firm, even though it would be justified for the risk-neutral firm. The risk-averse firm under this analysis would produce 2 units as indicated under the prior analysis and would decline the additional information. The risk-neutral firm, however, would obtain the additional information and produce either 2 or 3 units depending upon the information received.

Therefore, to achieve a good understanding of the supply side of many markets, we have seen some evidence that it is necessary to be aware of the risk preferences of the firms and whether additional information (which typically is imperfect) would be in their interest. In our simple example it was shown that even when a predictor appears to have a good record, it may not be worthwhile for some firms. Their decision under prior information may stand because the predictor is somewhat imperfect and the cost of the information may hit the risk-averse firm hard.

Computing the Posterior Probabilities

Up to this point we have not drawn attention to the probability trees and the table in the extreme lower-left part of Diagram 13.3. We need nothing more to compute the posterior probabilities, which we previously inserted in the main decision tree after Reading A and after Reading B. These are not decision trees but probability trees, which we read from left to right.

We begin by forming first an "initial" probability tree, as seen, that captures the prior probabilities of .80 and .20 on the "states" (recall that here the "states" refer to two price possibilities of $48 and $24) and also the record of Reading A and Reading B in predicting the states.

Thus, when the high price of $48 has occurred in the past, it is revealed to us that Reading A has occurred with a relative frequency of

.90. So essentially we say that if $48 exists in a future period there is a probability of .90 that we would get Reading A. The other possible reading given the same state is Reading B, with a probability of .10. (Remember that probabilities must sum to 1.00.)

Analogously, the record of the predictor shows that when $24 existed, Reading A occurred with a relative frequency of only .15 and Reading B with a relative frequency of .85. This is the basis for the probabilities of .15 and .85 placed on the respective readings when a $24 price occurs.

Given the appropriate probabilities on all of the branches of the initial probability tree, we can multiply the probabilities through the branches to obtain the so-called joint probabilities, which we place at the tips of the branches of the initial tree, and then move them to the body of the associated table (with "states" at the top and "readings" at the side). These joint probabilities represent the probability of both events occurring and illustrate the use of the "multiplication" rule.

The "addition" rule of probability permits us to sum the joint probabilities lying in each row, giving us the probabilities at the margin of the table. Each of these probabilities at the margin of the table gives us the probability of a reading, namely .75 on Reading A and .25 on Reading B.

The final step (which we repeat four times) in computing each of the posterior probabilities is illustrated by the computation of the posterior probability of $48 given that Reading A is obtained.

We form the ratio of the joint probability of Reading A and $48 (which is .72 from the table) to the probability of receiving Reading A (which is .75 and is shown at the Reading A margin of the table). Thus, we have the following:

Posterior probability of $48 given Reading A = .72/.75 = .96

An interpretation is this: Out of 100 times we would in this setting tend to get Reading A 75 times, and 72 out of the 75 times $48 would be the price associated with this reading. Thus, .72/.75 = .96.

This result and others similarly obtained are placed in a "reverse" tree (as seen in the lower-left section of Diagram 13.3), which places the reading probabilities from the table's margin on the first branches of the tree (from the left) followed by posterior probabilities on the prices of $48 and $24.

The other posterior probabilities are computed as follows:

The posterior probability of $24 given Reading A = .03/.75 = .04.
The posterior probability of $48 given Reading B = .08/.25 = .32.
The posterior probability of $24 given Reading B = .17/.25 = .68.

Probabilities of these prices are the posterior probabilities after each reading that we incorporated into the main decision tree, along with the probabilities of the readings. We then analyzed the optimal decision after each reading and, ultimately, the expected value of using the additional information.

In the case of firms and decision makers, there appears to be a general assessment that in intuitive decision making, when such explicit computational assistance is not available, there is still an attempt to combine prior information with additional information in this logical way, but complexity often interferes. Therefore, we see—even in the simple example used here for purposes of illustration—that explicit quantitative procedures can enhance attempts at rational decision making by firms and others when prior information and access to additional information are possible.

Problems

13.1 Let us consider a single change in the example in Diagram 13.3 on price uncertainty. The change is in the initial (prior) probabilities of the possible product prices assumed. Instead of the .80 and .20 prior probabilities on the product prices of $48 and $24, the prior probabilities are .50 and .50.

(a) For a risk-neutral firm in this setting, what is the optimal output and its expected profit under prior information only?

(b) For the specific risk-averse firm portrayed, what is the optimal output and its expected utility under prior information only? Compare and discuss the optimal acts for the risk-neutral and risk-averse firms.

(c) Given the availability of the same predictor shown in the example in Diagram 13.3, obtain the posterior probabilities of the prices $48 and $24 after Reading A and after Reading B. Compare and discuss the different posterior probabilities obtained compared to those in the example in Diagram 13.3.

Box 13.1

Government Policies That Reduce Uncertainty for Firms, Consumers, and Various Government Units

- A strong system of justice and security.
- Tax exemption for nonprofit institutions that generate and maintain mutual trust, cooperation, and community well-being.
- Economic and statistical reporting by the Department of Commerce (especially the Bureau of the Census), the Bureau of Labor Statistics; the Department of Agriculture, and other units.
- Health, safety, and environmental monitoring and control by the Food and Drug Administration, the Federal Aviation Administration, the Environmental Protection Agency, the Department of Agriculture, the National Weather Service, the Federal Deposit Insurance Corporation, and other units.

(d) For the risk-neutral firm, obtain the optimal output and its expected profit after the possible receipt of Reading A. Compare the optimal output with that obtained under prior information alone in (a).

(e) For the risk-averse firm, what is the optimal output and its expected utility after Reading A? Compare with the optimal output obtained under prior information alone in (b).

(f) For the risk-neutral firm, obtain the optimal output and its expected profit after the receipt of Reading B. Compare this output with that obtained under prior information alone in (a).

(g) For the risk-averse firm, what is the optimal output and its expected utility after Reading B? Compare this output with that obtained under prior information alone in (b).

(h) Obtain for the risk-neutral firm the expected profit *using* a reading from the predictor and compare it with the optimal expected profit under prior information alone. Should the risk-neutral firm obtain the information? Discuss.

(i) Obtain for the risk-averse firm the expected utility *using* a reading and compare it with the optimal expected utility under prior information alone. Should the risk-averse firm obtain the information? Discuss.

14

Multiple Objectives and Environmental Policy

Up to this time we have assumed that higher total profit was the single objective of the firm. This was also true as we considered a risk-averse firm in a previous chapter. In that discussion, however, we noted that for such a firm under uncertainty each dollar of profit that might be gained or lost was not equal in importance.

We return now to the assumption of certainty, but we face the added complexity that arises when an objective in addition to total profit may be relevant. A commonly occurring case is one where the firm sees a larger amount of total revenue, at least for some short period of time, as being very important, perhaps more important than higher total profit. Later we shall begin to see how environmental objectives can be incorporated into the analysis as well.

In Diagram 14.1 we return to our familiar firm, but with an additional constraint imposed by the firm that requires total profit for the period to be at least $20, while total revenue is the objective to be maximized.

In Diagram, 14.1 we focus on the direct solution of the short-run problem with Resource 2 completely variable. But now total revenue (TR) is to be maximized with total profit before fixed cost (TPBFC) being placed down with the constraints.

The coefficients in the TR objective function in this direct solution procedure are comprised simply of the unit revenues from the output by each process, but the TPBFC function is now a "greater-than" inequality among the constraints, and its coefficients incorporate for each process the unit revenue and the variable Resource 2 cost per unit.

With the current minimum TPBFC of $20 specified, a graphical solu-

Diagram 14.1 **Multiple Objectives in a Firm Where Total Revenue Is Maximized Subject to a Minimum Total Profit Constraint**
(Res 2 variable)

Max TR $= 24X_1 + 24X_2$

Subject to $2X_1 + 3X_2 \leq 6$ (Res 1)

$4X_1 + 14X_2 \geq 20$ (current lower limit on TPBFC and param from 0 to 28)

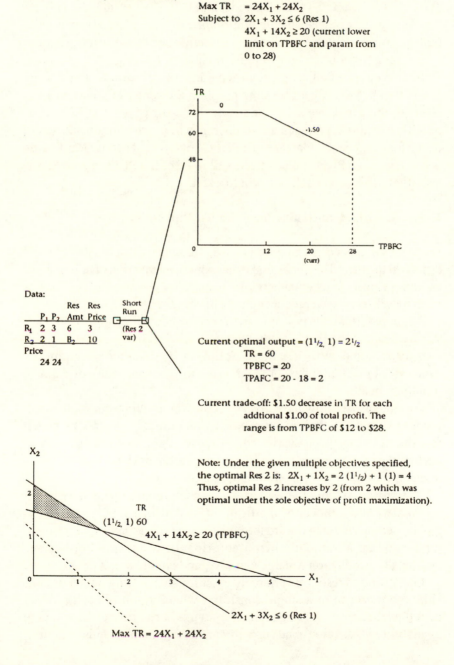

Data:

	P_1	P_2	Res Amt	Res Price	
R_1	2	3	6	3	Short Run
R_2	2	1	B_2	10	(Res 2 var)
Price					
	24	24			

Current optimal output = $(1^1/_2, 1) = 2^1/_2$
TR = 60
TPBFC = 20
TPAFC = 20 - 18 = 2

Current trade-off: $1.50 decrease in TR for each addtional $1.00 of total profit. The range is from TPBFC of $12 to $28.

Note: Under the given multiple objectives specified, the optimal Res 2 is: $2X_1 + 1X_2 = 2 (1^1/_2) + 1 (1) = 4$
Thus, optimal Res 2 increases by 2 (from 2 which was optimal under the sole objective of profit maximization).

tion appears in the lower part of Diagram 14.1 showing the optimal program to be (1½, 1) with a total output of 2½ units and total revenue (TR) of $60. The TPBFC is $20 and TPAFC is $2. The specified objective TR was maximized and the minimum TPBFC of $20 was just satisfied. Of course, for larger problems we would need the software program.

Because firms often contemplate raising or lowering the minimum TPBFC to be specified, we proceed to parameterize the minimum TPBFC from $0 to $28. This generates the graph in the center of Diagram 14.1.

From the graph we see the current trade-off of TR for TPBFC to be −$1.50, indicating that a $1.50 decrease in the maximum TR would occur for every $1.00 increase in TPBFC specified. That trade-off value is constant for TPBFC values from $12 to $28. If TPBFC above $28 is specified, no feasible solution would exist.

Environmental Constraints and the Multiproduct Firm

Environmental concerns create a growing influence on optimal output decisions in the firm. The imposition by law or moral sanction of minimum or maximum attribute requirements with respect to the total of all products or of some subset of such product outputs of firms is not uncommon.

These requirements typically focus on the control of some of the adverse effects of the firm's production activities with regard to (1) pollution in the air or water or noise pollution; (2) energy consumption, especially by automobiles; or (3) the risk of personal injury or damage to human health.

Fortunately, we now have a very direct way to represent such a situation of firms with their many products, numerous processes by which to produce each product, various resource availabilities and their use by each of the processes, and also a way to represent such attribute requirements imposed to control environmental quality.

To indicate roughly the way in which such requirements may be incorporated into a model of the firm, let us consider a very simple example, perhaps looking toward the construction of a much larger practical model for an automobile manufacturing firm considering various amounts of production of large cars, X_1, and small cars, X_2.

Many limited resources typically exist for such a firm, but let us consider the presence of a single constraint where a unit of each product uses the resource at the same rate of 2 hours. Furthermore, the resource availability is assumed to be currently at 12 (say, in thousands of hours):

$$2X_1 + 2X_2 \leq 12.$$

A second constraint illustrates the way in which an energy-consumption constraint might be imposed on the firm with regard to the energy consumption attribute of its total output. Suppose the average fuel consumption for all vehicles produced is required to be at least 24 miles per gallon. This gives rise to a constraint in the following initial form (We assume the larger car fuel consumption is 16 miles per gallon, whereas for the small car it is 32):

$$16X_1 + 32X_2 \geq 24(X_1 + X_2).$$

Collecting terms, we have the constraint $-8X_1 + 8X_2 \geq 0$, which we include with the resource constraint as well as a profit objective function (each coefficient representing, say, thousands of dollars before fixed costs):

$$\text{Maximize TPBFC} = 8X_1 + 4X_2$$

Subject to:

$$2X_1 + 2X_2 \leq 12 \text{ (Resource)}$$
$$-8X_1 + 8X_2 \geq 0 \text{ (Aggregate fuel consumption attribute).}$$

The optimal-profit output program is $(X_1, X_2) = (3000, 3000)$, that is, equal amounts of the two products, with a total profit (before fixed costs) of $36,000,000. This problem can be solved graphically, as in Diagram 14.2, but larger problems would, of course, require the simplex method.

In the absence of the fuel consumption constraint, the optimal output would be $(X_1, X_2) = (6000, 0)$. Only the larger car would be produced, resulting in total profit (before fixed costs) of $48,000,000. (Naturally we are assuming no change in product prices or any possible insufficient demand at higher output levels.) Thus, the fuel consumption constraint would, under assumed conditions, reduce total profit by $12,000,000.

The Effect of Changing the Fuel Consumption Requirements

Additionally, we can illustrate, as in Diagram 14.2, the effect on optimal total profit of varying the fuel consumption constraint from its assumed

Diagram 14.2   **Environmental Constraints and a Multiproduct Firm**

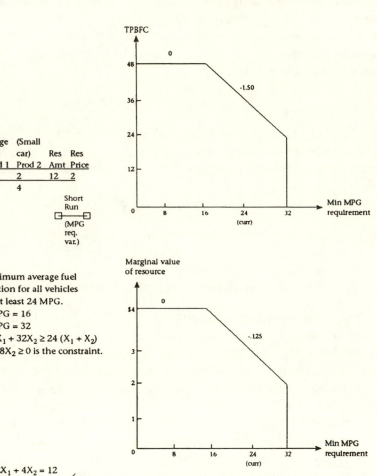

Max TPBFC $= 8X_1 + 4X_2$
Subject to $2X_1 + 2X_2 \leq 12$ (Resource)
                   $-8X_1 + 8X_2 \geq 0$ (Min MPG requirement)

Data:

	(Large car) Prod 1	(Small car) Prod 2	Res Amt	Res Price
R_1	2	2	12	2
Profit	8	4		
BFC			Short Run	

(MPG req. var.)

Also, minimum average fuel consumption for all vehicles must be at least 24 MPG.
Prod 1 MPG = 16
Prod 2 MPG = 32
Thus, $16X_1 + 32X_2 \geq 24 (X_1 + X_2)$
or $-8X_1 + 8X_2 \geq 0$ is the constraint.

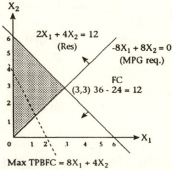

X_2

$2X_1 + 4X_2 = 12$
(Res)

$-8X_1 + 8X_2 = 0$
(MPG req.)

FC
(3,3) 36 - 24 = 12

Max TPBFC $= 8X_1 + 4X_2$

For each unit increase in the min MPG requirement from 16 to 32, TPBFC (and TPAFC) decrease by $1.50. Thus, the current TPAFC of $12 would decrease to $10.50 if the min MPG requirement were increased to 25. Additionally, the marginal value of the resource decreases by $.125 for each unit increase in the min MPG requirement from 16 to 32. Thus, the current marginal value of $3.00 would fall to $2.875 if the requirement were raised to 25 from the current 24.

current amount of 24. For every unit increase from a minimum requirement of 24 miles per gallon for the entire output to 32, the optimal total profit is reduced by $1,500,000. Also, Diagram 14.2 shows that the lowering of the minimum requirement by each unit from 24 to 16 would raise optimal profit by $1,500,000 for each unit decrease in the fuel consumption requirement.

Another relationship of interest is the way in which the fuel consumption requirement affects the values of resources that the firm uses in its production. Generally, when the value of resources to the firm rises there is an increased incentive to acquire more of those resources through investment or acquisition.

As the fuel consumption requirement in our example is raised from the assumed current amount of 24 to 32, we see in Diagram 14.2 that the current marginal value of the resource to the firm (which is $3,000,000) falls by $125,000 for every unit increase in the fuel consumption requirement. This drop in the "current marginal contribution to profit" of the resource as the fuel consumption requirement is raised would tend to lead to reduced investment spending on this resource.

In summary, we note that when public policy provides for the imposition of minimum or maximum product attributes on the output of the firm, a very direct representation of such constraints is made possible by the procedures we have outlined. Not only can an optimal output program for the firm be identified under current public policy, but also the effect of changes in public policy on the firm's output programs, their profitability, and finally the effect on resource values and the incentive for further investment in those resources.

Problems

14.1 Consider a change in the example firm with multiple objectives portrayed in Diagram 14.1. Now, a new lower limit on the TPBFC (total profit before fixed cost) is presented. Instead of the current $20, it is $24. All other data remain the same, including the complete variability of Resource 2 and the maximization of TR (total revenue).

(a) Obtain the optimal output program and the optimal total output.

(b) Obtain the optimal total revenue.

Box 14.1

Environmental Policies

The free-market system works reasonably well when buyers and sellers take into account the consequences to themselves of actions they might take. However, numerous instances abound where the actions taken by firms or consumers result in significant consequences to "third parties"—that is, to parties external to the transactions.

Such third-party consequences have been termed "externalities." These consequences may be beneficial to others, such as in some educational decisions, or they may by harmful to others, as in actions that adversely affect the environment.

If a firm's operations pollute the air or soil, thus affecting others, these consequences may not be taken into account by the firm. Hence, expenses of cleaning up or avoiding the pollution may not be borne directly by the firm and would require public intervention in the form of taxation or direct control to remedy or stop the pollution.

In the United States, public policy intervention has occurred mainly in the form of the Clean Air Act (1963, 1970, 1990), which established direct controls on standards of emission of pollutants. Various provisions included in the act were aimed at achieving progress in incorporating these consequences into decisions on economic activities that generate the pollution.

(c) Obtain the total profit before fixed cost (TPBFC) and the total profit after fixed cost (TPAFC) of the optimal program.
(d) Indicate the effect of the increased lower limit on TPBFC on the optimal amount of Resource 2 to hire. How does it compare with the optimal Resource 2 amount under the sole objective of profit maximization? Discuss.

15

Multiple Products and Multiple Processes

Let us illustrate here an extension of our earlier examples to take into account more than one product as well as the existence of more than one process by which one or more products might be made. Later we shall examine the case where one product also serves as an input to another product within the same firm.

First, we choose an example where a firm considers two products, Product A and Product B, as seen in the data table in Diagram 15.1. Product A can be produced by only one process, Process 1, and its output is represented by X_1. Product B can be produced by two processes, Process 2 and Process 3. We represent the output by Process 2 by X_2 and the output by Process 3 by X_3. Thus, the output of Product B in any program will simply be the sum of X_2 and X_3.

From the data table in Diagram 15.1, we form the problem for the immediate period as we did in the simpler examples. The coefficients in the objective function will be given by the product prices. Here, with two products we have two prices, $72 for Product A and $44 for Product B. This gives us two different coefficients in the objective function, even in the immediate period.

We construct the "less than" resource constraints as before, attaching the rates of use of the resources to the appropriate variables and specifying that the right-hand sides indicate the availabilities of the resources.

Because we have three variables in the problem, we go to the LINDO software and show the solution in Diagram 15.1.

The optimal program appears in the X-variables; thus, to obtain the amount of each product output we need the sum of the output of the product made by all processes involved in a specific product. The optimal program $(X_1, X_2, X_3) = (6,0,60)$ indicates an output of 6 of Product

Diagram 15.1   **Multiple Products A and B in the Firm With Multiple Processes Available for Product B**

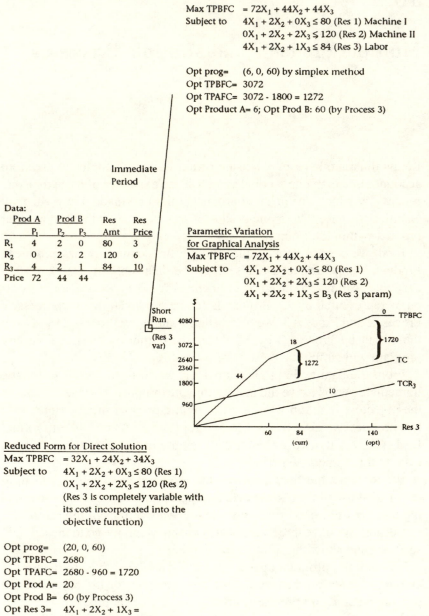

Max TPBFC $= 72X_1 + 44X_2 + 44X_3$
Subject to $4X_1 + 2X_2 + 0X_3 \leq 80$ (Res 1) Machine I
$0X_1 + 2X_2 + 2X_3 \leq 120$ (Res 2) Machine II
$4X_1 + 2X_2 + 1X_3 \leq 84$ (Res 3) Labor

Opt prog=   (6, 0, 60) by simplex method
Opt TPBFC= 3072
Opt TPAFC= 3072 - 1800 = 1272
Opt Product A= 6; Opt Prod B: 60 (by Process 3)

Immediate
Period

Data:

Prod A	Prod B		Res	Res
P_1	P_2	P_3	Amt	Price
R_1 4	2	0	80	3
R_2 0	2	2	120	6
R_3 4	2	1	84	10
Price 72	44	44		

Parametric Variation
for Graphical Analysis
Max TPBFC $= 72X_1 + 44X_2 + 44X_3$
Subject to $4X_1 + 2X_2 + 0X_3 \leq 80$ (Res 1)
$0X_1 + 2X_2 + 2X_3 \leq 120$ (Res 2)
$4X_1 + 2X_2 + 1X_3 \leq B_3$ (Res 3 param)

Short
Run
☐
(Res 3
var)

Reduced Form for Direct Solution
Max TPBFC $= 32X_1 + 24X_2 + 34X_3$
Subject to $4X_1 + 2X_2 + 0X_3 \leq 80$ (Res 1)
$0X_1 + 2X_2 + 2X_3 \leq 120$ (Res 2)
(Res 3 is completely variable with
its cost incorporated into the
objective function)

Opt prog=   (20, 0, 60)
Opt TPBFC= 2680
Opt TPAFC= 2680 - 960 = 1720
Opt Prod A= 20
Opt Prod B= 60 (by Process 3)
Opt Res 3= $4X_1 + 2X_2 + 1X_3 =$
4 (20) + 2 (0) + 1 (60) = 140

A and 60 of Product B. All 60 units of Product B would be produced by Process 3. None would be produced by Process 2.

In the short-run analysis (middle of Diagram 15.1) we parameterize the Resource 3 amount, which generates the TPBFC graph against Resource 3 amounts on the horizontal axis. Because the parameterization does not include the cost of Resource 3, we insert its cost in the graphical analysis as well as the fixed cost of $960. This gives us the total cost graph (TC).

The optimal Resource 3 amount is seen to be an input of 140, much above the current Resource 3 amount of 84. At the optimal Resource 3 amount, TPAFC would rise to $1720 from the current $1272.

Although we have not constructed the graph of the marginal contribution of Resource 3, we can obtain its values from the slopes of the TPBFC graph. Recall that it provides the firm's demand curve of Resource 3 and indicates quickly the optimal Resource 3 amount for the firm at various possible Resource 3 prices. For example, if the Resource 3 price were to rise from its current $10 to a price somewhat above $18, the optimal Resource 3 amount for the firm would fall to 60. The entire market demand curve for Resource 3 is essentially comprised of the summation of all of the individual firms' demand curves for Resource 3.

At the bottom of Diagram 15.1 we undertake the procedure to obtain the direct solution to the short-run problem where Resource 3 is now treated as being completely variable, with its cost incorporated into the objective function.

The coefficients in the objective function now reflect the Resource 3 cost per unit by each process, which permits us to drop the Resource 3 constraint from our linear programming formation.

The optimal program is $(X_1, X_2, X_3) = (20, 0, 60)$, indicating an output of 20 units of Product A and 60 units of Product B. All of Product B would be produced by Process 3. The optimal TPBFC in this formulation is $2680 and TPAFC is again found to be $1720 ($2680 − $960, the fixed cost of Resource 1 and Resource 2). From this formulation, too, we find the optimal Resource 3 amount to be 140 when we substitute the optimal program into the Resource 3 equation.

Multiple Products: The Case Where One Product Is an Input for Another Product

For firms producing more that one product it is not uncommon for one or more of the products that it places on the market also to be used internally as a component (that is, as an input) for another product in its very own production activities.

An example might be that of a firm producing small electric motors for sale and also furnaces used to heat homes. Each furnace needs one of the electric motors. Therefore, there is the need to include in the analysis a requirement (a constraint) that asserts that the number of electric motors produced must be at least as large as the number of furnaces produced and that each furnace produced requires one of the motors.

A very simple example of such a firm is illustrated in Diagram 15.2. Two products are produced, but Product 1 not only uses Resource 1 and Resource 2 but also requires one unit of Product 2 as an input. We attempt to show this in the data table along with other relevant information.

The novel aspect of this situation is that, in addition to the resource constraints, a constraint is needed that captures the requirement that one unit of Product 2 is needed as an input for every unit of Product 1.

Thus, we assert the requirement that $X_2 \geq X_1$. And, rearranging the terms so we have all the variables on the left-hand side, we have $-X_1 + X_2 \geq 0$. As seen in Diagram 15.2, we include it with the resource constraints.

Also, the coefficients in the objective function need to reflect the sacrifice in profit on each unit of Product 2 output that serves as an input to Product 1. Because $12 of profit is lost in this way, it is necessary to subtract $12 from the $36 price for Product 1 appearing in the data table. This reveals a coefficient of $24 for Product 1 and a coefficient of $12 for Product 2.

We see a current optimal program of (1,3) in the graphic solution in the lower-left portion of Diagram 15.2. We plot the $24 TPBFC graph as a dashed line, and in optimizing fashion move it out to the extreme corner point of the feasible region.

The current optimal program has a TPBFC of $60, but total fixed costs of $56 give a TPAFC of $4. However, short-run parameter variation of Resource 2 reveals the optimal Resource 2 amount to be 8 instead of the current 12, with a TPAFC of $8 rather than $4.

Problems

15.1   In Diagram 15.2, the example firm produces two products, Product 2 being required as an input for Product 1. Consider the effect

Diagram 15.2   **Optimal Output of a Product That Is Required as an Input for Another Product**

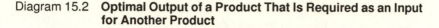

$$\text{Max TPBFC} = 24X_1 + 12X_2$$
$$\text{Subject to} \quad 2X_1 + 2X_2 \leq 8 \text{ (Res 1)}$$
$$6X_1 + 2X_2 \leq 12 \text{ (Res 2 and param 0 to 20)}$$
$$-X_1 + X_2 \geq 0 \text{ (Min output of Prod 2)}$$

Data:

	Prod 1	Prod 2	Res Amt	Res Price
R_1	2	2	8	1
R_2	6	2	12	4
Prod 2 Input	1	0	-	-
Prod Prices	36	12		

Prod 1 Unit profit = 24: (36 - 12)
Prod 2 Unit profit = 12
TPBFC   = $36X_1 + 12(X_2 - X_1)$
                                   = $24X_1 + 12X_2$

Current optimal program = (1,3)
TPBFC = 60
TPAFC = 60 - 56 = 4

Optimal Resource 2 input if variable
as in above parameterization = 8
TPBFC = 48
TPAFC = 48 - 40 = 8

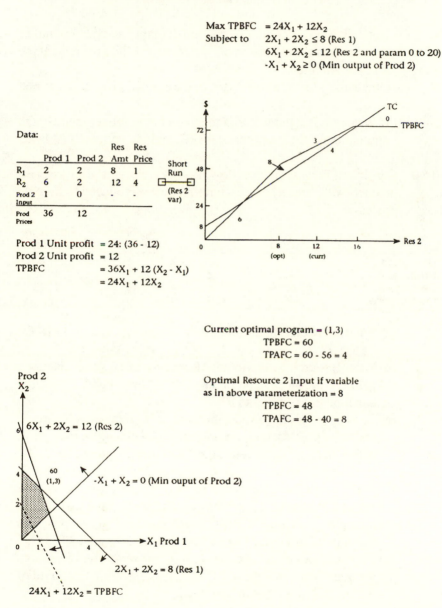

of a single change in the example. Now Product 2 has a unit profit before fixed cost of $6 instead of $12.

(a) Obtain the current optimal program of output and the amount of each product if the Resource 1 and Resource 2 inputs hold at the original amounts.
(b) Obtain the TPBFC and TPAFC of the optimal program obtained in (a).
(c) If Resource 2 is parameterized over a broad range, identify the optimal output, the optimal TPBFC, and the optimal TPAFC.

15.2 Consider a firm with the following data table as it produces two products with three resources. Each product is produced by a single process.

	Product 1	Product 2	Resource amount	Resource price
Resource 1	0	2	6	$1.00
Resource 2	4	2	12	$ .50
Resource 3	4	4	16	$ .40
Product price	$4	$8		

(a) What is the current optimal feasible program and its TPBFC? Its TPAFC?
(b) Vary Resource 1 individually from zero to 12 and construct a graph of the slopes and breakpoints of the TPBFC (which at this moment is equal to TR).
(c) To your graph in (b) add the total cost graph of Resource 1 and show the Resource 1 input that would maximize total profit before taking into account the fixed costs of Resource 2 and Resource 3. Then, include on your graph the total fixed cost of Resource 2 and Resource 3 (along with the total cost of the varying Resource 1), giving a grand total fixed cost graph that, along with the TPBFC graph obtained in (b), provides the optimal amount of Resource 1 and the optimal TPAFC.
(d) Compare the current optimal TPAFC and the current Resource 1 amount with the optimal TPAFC and the optimal amount of Resource 1 when it can be varied.

15.3 The following data table for a firm includes data on a possible new Product 3 being considered.

	Product 1	Product 2	New Product 3	Resource amount	Resource price
Resource 1	4	4	0	240	$3
Resource 2	0	4	4	160	$2
Product price	$16	$24	$12		

(a) If only Product 1 and Product 2 are considered, obtain the optimal program and its TPBFC and TPAFC.

(b) If production of Product 3 is considered as well as that of Product 1 and Product 2, what is the optimal program and its TPBFC and TPAFC?

(c) Discuss any changes in the optimal program and the optimal TPBFC and TPAFC as a result of Product 3.

15.4 A firm makes backpacks and raincoats, each by a separate but single process. A preliminary data table below includes five resource inputs, with only Resource 1 (machine hours) and Resource 2 (labor hours) fixed in amounts for an upcoming period. All other inputs are completely variable during this period.

	Product 1 Back-packs	Product 2 Rain-coats	Resource amount available	Resource price per unit of input
Resource 1 (machine hours)	4 hours	2 hours	160 hours	$ 2 per hour
Resource 2 (labor hours)	4 hours	4 hours	240 hours	$20 per hour
Resource 3 (cloth in yards)	1 yard	2 yards	B_3 in hours	$ 4 per yard
Resource 4 (administrative support in hours)	2 hours	½ hour	B_4 in hours	$ 8 per hour
Resource 5 (packaging in pounds)	¼ pound	¼ pound	B_5 in pounds	$16 per pound
Product price	$120	$80		

(a) Obtain the variable cost per unit for Product 1 and for Product 2 based on the prices and rates of usage of Resources 3, 4, and 5.

(b) Obtain the TPBFC per unit of Product 1 and of Product 2.

(c) Form a linear programming model of the firm's decision based on the information in the data table above and your computations in (a) and (b).

(d) Solve for the current optimal program and its TPBFC and TPAFC using LINDO or the graphic method.

(e) After obtaining the current solution in (d), parameterize Resource 2 fully from zero to 500 hours and construct a graph showing the slopes and breakpoints of the TPBFC. Identify the current Resource 2 input and the optimal Resource 2 input if Resource 2 can be varied. Discuss your findings.

(f) Suppose a financial constraint arises in the acquisition of Resource 3 (cloth). Resource 3 for a new period is not now completely variable, as in the original data table, and an additional constraint inequality must appear in the linear programming formulation developed in (c). The financial limit is $160. Create the new formulation, which should reflect the requirement that only programs incurring $160 or less on cloth expenditures are feasible.

(g) What is the new optimal program and its TPBFC and TPAFC?

(h) Discuss any changes in the optimal program and the optimal TPBFC and TPAFC.

16

Multiple Locations of Production and Transportation Costs

In this chapter, we introduce the important problem of multiple locations of production of a product that is sold to buyers at many locations. Differing production costs at various locations need to be taken into account as well as the transportation costs of the product output to the buyers. The first problem is identifying, in the immediate period, the optimal flow of the product from each of the producing locations to each of the buyers' locations. Then, given some time, as in the short-run period when some inputs can change, the main problem is determining where expansion of output should occur given an increase in demand at one or more locations.

The Immediate Problem of Optimal Product Flow From Producing Origins to Buyers in Different Regions

A very important aspect of efficiency and profitability in the firm has to do with the location of its production facilities relative to the location of the buyers of its products.

The buyers of the firm's products usually already exist in various locations throughout a country or throughout the world. Their location, however, can have a great effect on the costs of transporting the products to the buyers. Also, production costs vary from location to location owing to differing costs of raw materials, labor, and other resources.

In Diagram 16.1 we assemble in a flow diagram some of the main elements necessary for the analysis of such problems. The main concern here is the minimization of cost and how much of the output should go

Diagram 16.1 **Transportation Costs Incorporated in the Analysis of Optimal Product Flow and the Location of Facilities for a Product**

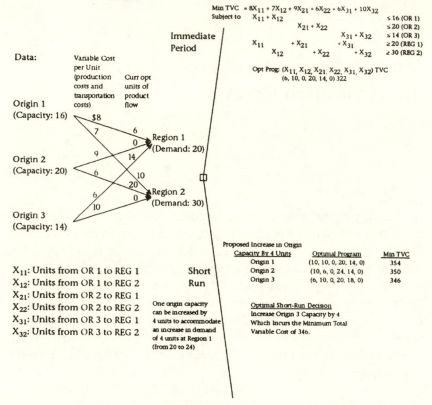

Min TVC $= 8X_{11} + 7X_{12} + 9X_{21} + 6X_{22} + 6X_{31} + 10X_{32}$

Subject to

$$X_{11} + X_{12} \qquad\qquad\qquad \leq 16 \text{ (OR 1)}$$
$$X_{21} + X_{22} \qquad\qquad \leq 20 \text{ (OR 2)}$$
$$X_{31} + X_{32} \leq 14 \text{ (OR 3)}$$
$$X_{11} \quad + X_{21} \quad + X_{31} \qquad \geq 20 \text{ (REG 1)}$$
$$X_{12} \quad + X_{22} \quad + X_{32} \geq 30 \text{ (REG 2)}$$

Opt Prog: $(X_{11}, X_{12}, X_{21}, X_{22}, X_{31}, X_{32})$ TVC
(6, 10, 0, 20, 14, 0) 322

Immediate Period

Data:

Variable Cost per Unit (production costs and transportation costs) / Curr opt units of product flow

Origin 1 (Capacity: 16) $8

Origin 2 (Capacity: 20)

Origin 3 (Capacity: 14)

Region 1 (Demand: 20)

Region 2 (Demand: 30)

X_{11}: Units from OR 1 to REG 1
X_{12}: Units from OR 1 to REG 2
X_{21}: Units from OR 2 to REG 1
X_{22}: Units from OR 2 to REG 2
X_{31}: Units from OR 3 to REG 1
X_{32}: Units from OR 3 to REG 2

Short Run

One origin capacity can be increased by 4 units to accommodate an increase in demand of 4 units at Region 1 (from 20 to 24)

Proposed Increase in Origin Capacity By 4 Units

	Optimal Program	Min TVC
Origin 1	(10, 10, 0, 20, 14, 0)	354
Origin 2	(10, 6, 0, 24, 14, 0)	350
Origin 3	(6, 10, 0, 20, 18, 0)	346

Optimal Short-Run Decision
Increase Origin 3 Capacity by 4
Which Incurs the Minimum Total
Variable Cost of 346.

from each producing location (each "origin") to each "region" where the buyers are located.

Our example is a firm producing a single product at three already established locations: Origin 1, Origin 2, and Origin 3. Its buyers are located in two different regions, Region 1 and Region 2.

Current estimates of demand are 20 units in Region 1 and 30 in Region 2. The capacity of production is 16 at Origin 1, 20 at Origin 2, and 14 at Origin 3. This data is recorded in the flow diagram in Diagram 16.1. Also shown is the optimal product flow from each origin to each region. How this optimal program is obtained is illustrated in the following paragraphs.

First, we need the unit variable cost of production at each origin to which we add the transportation cost as the product goes to each region. We record this data on the branches of the flow diagram.

The data we have gathered can be organized into linear programming form as seen in Diagram 16.1. The variables refer to the amount of product flow from each origin to each region. Consequently, two-digit subscripts are used for the variables to represent the flow of a product from a specific origin to a specific region. Thus, X_{11} represents the flow from Origin 1 to Region 1, X_{12} the flow from Origin 1 to Region 2, and so forth.

The coefficients in the objective function represent the unit variable costs, which are assembled in the flow diagram. The constraints are essentially statements pertaining to each origin capacity and each region demand. Each origin has a separate capacity constraint and each region has a separate demand constraint.

For example, the Origin 1 capacity constraint is simply $X_{11} + X_{12} \leq$ 16. It represents the requirement that the number of units produced and sent from Origin 1 (to all regions) cannot exceed 16.

All region demand constraints will be represented by "greater than" constraints as we specify that the flow to each region (from all origins) must at least satisfy the stated demand or exceed it. For example, for Region 1 the constraint is $X_{11} + X_{21} + X_{31} \geq 20$. The total from all origins must be equal to or exceed 20 units. We should note, too, that all of the variables appearing in the constraints implicitly will have a coefficient of 1 since we are simply summing the values of the variables in each constraint.

With this formulation shown in Diagram 16.1 we see by LINDO the optimal solution is: $(X_{11}, X_{12}, X_{21}, X_{22}, X_{31}, X_{32}) = (6, 10, 0, 20, 14, 0)$ with a total variable cost of $322.

The Optimal Location to Increase Capacity

Looking ahead, the firm sees an increase in demand occurring in Region 1 such that 24 units would be sold instead of only 20.

We can undertake an analysis to determine which origin capacity should be increased to satisfy the greater demand. Any of the three origin capacities can be increased by 4 units, and the question arises as to which will incur the lowest cost.

We return to our basic linear programming formulation in Diagram 16.1 and make some appropriate changes in the right-hand-side values. Now we have the case of two right-hand-side values changing simultaneously, so the simplest procedure is to solve a series of linear programming problems where each origin capacity is increased individually by

4 units (one at a time) along with the increase in Region 1 demand of 4 units.

The results of doing this are shown in Diagram 16.1. It is seen that of the three origins, total variable cost (TVC) is at a minimum if Origin 3 capacity is increased to satisfy the increase in Region 1 demand. The minimum TVC was found to be $346. Increasing each of the other origin capacities individually would incur a higher TVC.

We should note that the above analysis could also have been undertaken maximizing a profit-objective function instead of minimizing the cost-objective function.

If the product price is $11 in all regions, the profit-objective function would be as follows:

$$\text{Maximize TPBFC} = 3X_{11} + 4X_{12} + 2X_{21} + 5X_{22} + 5X_{31} + 1X_{32}.$$

The same optimal program would be obtained. Of course, as we have done before, the optimal TPAFC would be obtained by subtracting total fixed cost from the optimal TPBFC.

Problems

16.1　Consider a single change in the example firm in Diagram 16.1. Now, the transportation and production costs per unit from Origin 3 to Region 2 have been reduced from $10 to $5.

(a) Identify the new optimal program and its total variable cost (TVC).
(b) Discuss the effects of this transportation and production cost change on the optimal program and the minimum TVC.

16.2　In addition to the change in the transportation and production cost from Origin 3 to Region 2 in Problem 16.1, consider also a simultaneous change in the demand at Region 2 from 30 to 36 units. To accommodate this increase in demand at Region 2 any one of the three origin capacities can be increased by 6 units.

(a) Obtain the optimal program and its TVC if Origin 1 capacity is increased by 6 units to accommodate the change in demand.
(b) What is the optimal program and its TVC if the Origin 2 capacity is increased by 6 units instead?

Box 16.1

International Economic Policies

If a single world currency existed, along with a favorable political setting, and tariffs and subsidies were absent, the world economy would tend to resemble the large national economies such as that in the United States where the location of production of the many separate products and services would be largely dictated by production and distribution costs. And, indeed, with many European nations agreeing to a common currency and the U.S. trade policy moving toward more free-trade arrangements, the world economy edges toward a large free-trade area with a common currency.

But as long as tariffs and different currencies exist, distortions will be created. Industries in some countries will seek and obtain tariffs on imported products that threaten them. Also, individual nations may seek to serve their own short-run domestic purposes through separate monetary and exchange-rate policies.

But in a worldwide sense, the most efficient location of production (including transportation costs) serves to enhance welfare throughout the world.

Toward this end, each producing area in the world would seek those products that they would be most efficient in providing. It can be shown that, even if a given producing area is less efficient than all other areas, it will gain by focusing on the products in which it has the greatest relative efficiency. This is the essence of the law of comparative advantage.

A nation gains most by specializing in those things in which it has the greatest comparative advantage even if other nations are more efficient and have an absolute advantage in all products. An illustration might be drawn from the clothing industry. One country may be more efficient than others in both high-style and low-style clothing, but even though it is more efficient in both products, it would find it to its advantage to produce only the high-style clothing and leave it to a less efficient country to produce the low-style products.

(c) If Origin 3 capacity is increased by 6 units, what is the optimal program and its TVC?
(d) Which origin capacity should be increased by 6 units in order to minimize TVC?

Answers to Selected Problems

4.1 (a) Process 1 is more labor-intensive.

(b) Maximum total output for the immediate period is 2; the (0,2) program.

(c) Increases in output from varying Resource 2 are: 1 unit for Resource 2 inputs from 0 to 2; $1/5$ unit from 2 to 12; and 0 unit beyond 12.

(d) Resource 2 input of 2.

4.2 (a) Process 2 is more labor-intensive.

(b) Maximum total output in the immediate period is 4; the (2,2) program.

(c) Increases in output from varying Resource 2 are: 1 unit for Resource 2 inputs from 0 to 3; $1/3$ unit from 3 to 12; and 0 unit beyond 12.

(d) Resource 2 input of 3.

4.3 (a) Maximum total output in the immediate period is 2½; the (1,1½) program.

(b) Increases in output from varying Resource 2 are: ½ unit for Resource 2 inputs from 0 to 4; $1/8$ unit from 4 to 12; and 0 unit beyond 12.

(c) Resource 2 input of 4.

4.4 (a) Maximum total output in the immediate period is $2^1/_2$; the $(1^1/_2,1)$ program.

(b) Increases in output varying Resource 2 are: $^1/_2$ unit for Resource 2 inputs from 0 to 4; $^1/_8$ unit from 4 to 12; and 0 unit beyond 12.

(d) Resource 2 input of 4.

4.5 (a) Constant returns to scale occur for 100 percent increases in inputs from Resource 1 input of 3 and Resource 2 of 1. Output increases by 100 percent.

(b) Increasing returns to scale occur for 100 percent increases in inputs from Resource 1 of 6 and Resource 2 of 2. Output increases by more than 100 percent.

(c) Decreasing returns to scale occur for 100 percent increases in inputs from Resource 1 of 12 and Resource 2 of 4. Output increases by less than 100 percent.

5.1 (b) $26 is the optimal total profit in the immediate period.

(d) $36 is the optimal total profit in the short run.

(e) 12 is the optimal Resource 2 input in the short run.

(f) No.

5.2 (b) $66 is the optimal total profit in the immediate period.

(d) $84 is the optimal total profit in the short run.

(e) 12 is the optimal Resource 2 input in the short run.

(f) No.

5.3 (b) $236 is the optimal total profit in the immediate period.

(c) $240 is the optimal total profit in the short run.

(d) 12 is the optimal Resource 2 input in the short run.

(e) No, the optimal resource input is greater.

5.4   (b) $42 is the optimal total profit in the immediate period.

(c) $54 is the optimal total profit in the short run.

(d) 4 is the optimal Resource 2 input in the short run.

(e) No, the optimal resource input is smaller.

6.1   (a) The optimal total profit in the short run is $36 with an output of 4.

6.2   (a) The optimal total profit in the short run is $84 with an output of 6.

6.3   (a) The optimal total profit in the short run is $240 with an output of 3.

6.4   (a) The optimal total profit in the short run is $54 with an output of 2.

7.1   (a) MR_2 Cost is constant at $11. MR_2 Contribution is $60 from Resource 2 of 0 to 2; $12 from 2 to 12; $0 beyond 12.

(c) Optimal Resource 2 is 12 with TPAFC of $36.

(i) Optimal output is 4.

7.2   (a) MR_2 Cost is constant at $17. MR_2 Contribution is $48 from Resource 2 of 0 to 3; $16 from 3 to 12; $0 beyond 12.

(c) Optimal Resource 2 is 12 with TPAFC of $84.

(i) Optimal output is 6.

7.3   (a) MR_2 Cost is constant at $19. MR_2 Contribution is $80 from Resource 2 of 0 to 4; $20 from 4 to 12; $0 beyond 12.

(c) Optimal Resource 2 is 12 with TPAFC of $240.

(i) Optimal output is 3.

7.4 (a) MR_2 Cost is constant at $11. MR_2 Contribution is $32 from Resource 2 of 0 to 4; $8 from 4 to 12; $0 beyond 12.

(c) Optimal Resource 2 is 4 with TPAFC of $54.

(i) Optimal output is 2.

8.1 (a) (0,2); TPBFC is $120.

(b) TPAFC is $26.

(c) (0,0); TPBFC is $0; TPAFC is –$72.

(d) Slopes are $60, $12, and $0 with breakpoints at 2 and 12 for Resource 2.

(f) Optimal Resource 2 is 12 with TPAFC of $36.

(i) Max TPBFC $= 27X_1 + 49X_2$.

8.2 (a) (2,2); TPBFC is $192.

(b) TPAFC is $66.

(c) (0,0); TPBFC is $0; TPAFC is –$48.

(d) Slopes are $48, $16, and $0 with breakpoints at 3 and 12 for Resource 2.

(f) Optimal Resource 2 is 12 with TPAFC of $84.

(i) Max TPBFC $= 35X_1 + 22X_2$.

8.3 (a) (1,1½); TPBFC is $400.

(b) TPAFC is $236.

(c) (0,0); TPBFC is $0; TPAFC is –$12.

(d) Slopes are $80, $20, and $0, with breakpoints at 4 and 12 for Resource 2.

(f) Optimal Resource 2 is 12 with TPAFC of $240.

(i) Max TPBFC $= 122X_1 + 84X_2$.

8.4   (a) (1½,1); TPBFC is $160.

(b) TPAFC is $42.

(c) (0,0); TPBFC is $0; TPAFC is –$30.

(d) Slopes are $32, $8, and $0, with breakpoints at 4 and 12 for Resource 2.

(f) Optimal Resource 2 is 4 with TPAFC of $54.

(i) Max TPBFC $= 20X_1 + 42X_2$.

9.1   (a) In the immediate period the optimal program is (0,2); TPBFC is $150.

Optimal TPAFC in the immediate period is $56.

Slopes are $75, $15, and $0 with breakpoints at 2 and 12 for Resource 2.

Optimal Resource 2 in the short run is 12 with TPAFC of $96.

Optimal output in the short run is 4, the (4,0) program; TPAFC is $96.

In the short run, Max TPBFC $= 42X_1 + 64X_2$.

(b) In the immediate period the optimal output is 2, the (0,2) program; TPBFC is $120.

Optimal TPAFC in the immediate period is $20.

Slopes are $60, $12, and $0 with breakpoints at 2 and 12 for Resource 2.

In the short run, optimal Resource 2 is 2 with TPAFC of $20.

In the short run, optimal output is 2, the (0,2) program; TPAFC is $20.

In the short run, Max TPBFC = $18X_1 + 46X_2$.

9.2 (a) In the immediate period the optimal program is (2,2); TPBFC is $144.

Optimal TPAFC in the immediate period is $18.

Slopes are $36, $12, and $0 with breakpoints at 3 and 12 for Resource 2.

In the short run, optimal Resource 2 is 3 with TPAFC of $21.

In the short run, optimal output is 3, TPAFC is $21.

In the short run, Max TPBFC = $23X_1 + 10X_2$.

(b) In the immediate period the optimal program is (2,2); TPBFC is $192.

In the immediate period, TPAFC is $42.

Slopes are $48, $16, and $0, with breakpoints at 3 and 12 for variation of Resource 2.

In the short run, optimal Resource 2 is 3 with TPAFC of $45.

In the short run, optimal output is 3; TPAFC is $45.

In the short run, Max TPBFC = $31X_1 + 14X_2$.

9.3 (a) In the immediate period the optimal program is $(1,1^{1}/_{2})$; TPBFC is $360.

Optimal TPAFC in the immediate period is $196.

Slopes are $72, $18, and $0, with breakpoints at 4 and 12 for Resource 2.

Optimal Resource 2 in the short run is 4 with TPAFC of $200.

Optimal output in the short run is 2; the (2,0) program; TPAFC is $200.

In the short run, Max TPBFC $= 106X_{1} + 68X_{2}$.

(b) In the immediate period the optimal program is $(1,1^{1}/_{2})$; TPBFC is $400.

Optimal TPAFC in the immediate period is $212.

Slopes are $80, $20, and $0, with breakpoints at 4 and 12 for variation of Resource 2.

In the short run, optimal Resource 2 is 4 with TPAFC of $220.

In the short run, optimal output is 2; the (2,0) program; TPAFC is $220.

In the short run, Max TPBFC $= 116X_{1} + 72X_{2}$.

9.4 (a) In the immediate period the optimal program is $(1^{1}/_{2},1)$; TPBFC is $240.

Optimal TPAFC in the immediate period is $122.

Slopes are $48, $12, and $0, with breakpoints at 4 and 12 for Resource 2.

Optimal Resource 2 in the short run is 12 with TPAFC of $126.

Optimal output in the short run is 3; the (3,0) program; TPAFC is $126.

In the short run, Max TPBFC = $52X_1 + 74X_2$.

(b) In the immediate period the optimal program is $(1^1/_2, 1)$; TPBFC is $160.

Optimal TPAFC in the immediate period is $18.

Slopes are $32, $8, and $0, with breakpoints at 4 and 12 for variation of Resource 2.

In the short run, optimal Resource 2 is 4 with TPAFC of $42.

In the short run, optimal output is 2; the (0,2) program; TPAFC is $42.

In the short run, Max TPBFC = $8X_1 + 36X_2$.

10.1   In the immediate period the optimal output is 2, the (0,2) program; TPBFC is $120.

Optimal TPAFC in the immediate period is $26.

Slopes are $60, $9 $^9/_{19}$, and $0, with breakpoints at $2^1/_2$ and 12 for Resource 2.

In the short run, optimal Resource 2 is $2^1/_2$ with TPAFC of $50^1/_2$.

In the short run, optimal output is $2^1/_2$, the $(0,2^1/_2)$ program; TPAFC is $50^1/_2$.

In the short run, Max TPBFC = $27X_1 + 49X_2$.

10.2   In the immediate period the optimal output is $4^1/_2$, the $(3,1^1/_2)$ program; TPBFC is $162.

Optimal TPAFC in the immediate period is $48.

Slopes are $36, $9, and $0, with breakpoints at 4 and 12 for Resource 2.

In the short run, optimal Resource 2 is 4 with TPAFC of $52.

In the short run, optimal output is 4, the (4,0) program; TPAFC is $52.

In the short run, Max TPBFC $= 25X_1 + 14X_2$.

10.3 In the immediate period the optimal program is $(1^1/_3, 1)$; TPBFC is $373^1/_3$.

Optimal TPAFC in the immediate period is $209^1/_3$.

Slopes are $53^1/_3$, $26^2/_3$, and $0, with breakpoints at 6 and 12 for Resource 2.

In the short run, optimal Resource 2 is 12 with TPAFC of $240.

In the short run, optimal output is 3, the (0,3) program; TPAFC is $240.

In the short run, Max TPBFC $= 103X_1 + 84X_2$.

10.4 In the immediate period the optimal output is $2^3/_5$, the $(1^4/_5, ^4/_5)$ program; TPBFC is $166.40.

Optimal TPAFC in the immediate period is $48.40.

Slopes are $64, $6.40, and $0, with breakpoints at 2 and 12 for Resource 2.

In the short run, optimal Resource 2 is 2 with TPAFC of $76.

In the short run, optimal output is 2, the (0,2) program; TPAFC is $76.

In the short run, Max TPBFC $= 20X_1 + 53X_2$.

10.5   (a) In the immediate period the optimal output is 4, the (2,2) program; TPBFC is $336.

Optimal TPAFC in the immediate period is $36.

When Resource 2 is 0, the optimal program is (0,0); TPBFC is $0; TPAFC is –$144.

Slopes are $42, $14, and $0, with breakpoints at 6 and 24 for Resource 2.

In the short run, optimal Resource 2 is 24 with TPAFC of $48.

In the short run, Max TPBFC $= 32X_1 + 58X_2$.

(b) In the immediate period the optimal output is 5¼, the (¾,4½) program; TPBFC is $441.

Optimal TPAFC in the immediate period is $105.

When Resource 2 is 0, the optimal program is (0,0); TPBFC is $0; TPAFC is –$180.

Slopes are $42, $10½, and $0, with breakpoints at 10 and 30 for Resource 2.

In the short run, optimal Resource 2 is 10 with TPAFC of $110.

In the short run, optimal output is 5, the (0,5) program; TPAFC is $110.

In the short run, Max TPBFC $= 32X_1 + 58X_2$.

11.1   (a) The new optimal output is 3 instead of 6; TPAFC is $63 instead of $36.

(b) The new optimal Resource 2 is 3 instead of 12.

12.1 (a) In the short run when Resource 2 can be varied the new optimal output is 2, where TPAFC is at a maximum of $232. The higher unit cost of Resource 2 as more of it is acquired raises total costs sharply at higher output levels.

(b) The new optimal Resource 2 input is 4. Higher unit prices for Resource 2 as more of it is acquired causes optimal TPAFC to move to a lower input of Resource 2.

13.1 (a) For the risk-neutral firm, the optimal output is 2 units; the expected profit is $34.

(b) For the risk-averse firm, the optimal output is 2 units; the expected utility is .875.

(c) After Reading A, the posterior probabilities are .857 and .143. After Reading B, the posterior probabilities are .105 and .895.

(d) For the risk-neutral firm, after Reading A the optimal output is 3 units and the expected profit is $56.70.

(e) For the risk-averse firm, after Reading A the optimal output is 2 units and the expected utility is .956.

(f) For the risk-neutral firm, after Reading B the optimal output is 2 units and the expected profit is $14.04.

(g) For the risk-averse firm, after Reading B the optimal output is 2 units and the expected utility is .781.

(h) For the risk-neutral firm, the relevant expected profit using additional information (with a cost of $1) is $36.42. It is greater than the optimal expected profit of $34 under prior information alone. On this basis, the reading should be obtained after which the output decision should be made.

(i) For the risk-averse firm, the relevant expected utility using additional information (with a cost of $1) is .871. It is less than the optimal expected utility of .875 under prior information alone. On this basis, the additional information should not be obtained. Incurring the cost of information is not justified.

14.1 (a) The optimal output program is $(3/4, 1^1/2)$; optimal total output is $2^1/4$.

(b) Optimal total revenue is $54.

(c) The TPBFC of the optimal program is $24. The TPAFC of the optimal program is $6.

(d) The optimal amount of Resource 2 is 6. It was 2 under the sole objective of profit maximization.

15.1 (a) The current optimal program is $(1^1/2, 1^1/2)$, $1^1/2$ units of Product 1 and $1^1/2$ units of Product 2.

(b) Current optimal TPBFC is $6; TPAFC is $2.

(c) If Resource 2 is varied, the optimal output is (2,2) with TPBFC of $8; TPAFC of $0.

15.2 (a) The optimal program in the immediate period is (1,3); 1 unit of Product 1 and 3 of Product 2; TPBFC is $28; TPAFC is $9.60.

(b) Slopes are $3, $2, and $0, with breakpoints at 4 and 8 for Resource 1.

(c) When Resource 1 can be varied in the short run, the optimal Resource 1 is 8 with TPAFC of $11.60.

(d) In the immediate period with the current Resource 1 of 6, TPAFC is $9.60. In the short run when Resource 1 can be varied, the optimal Resource 1 is 8; TPAFC is $11.60.

15.3 (a) If only Product 1 and Product 2 are considered, the optimal program is (20,40); TPBFC is $1280; TPAFC is $240.

(b) If Product 3 is also considered, the optimal program is (60,0,40); TPBFC is $1440; TPAFC is $400.

(c) Product 3 edges out Product 2 even though the price of Product 3 is only half that of Product 2; its lack of use of Resource 1 frees Resource 1 for more of Product 1, and a resulting increase in TPAFC from $240 to $400.

15.4 (a) For Product 1, the variable cost per unit is $24; for Product 2 it is $16.

(b) For Product 1, the unit profit before fixed cost is $96; for Product 2 it is $64.

(c) Max TPBFC $= 96X_1 + 64X_2$

Subject to: $4X_1 + 2X_2 \leq 160$ (Res 1)

   $4X_1 + 4X_2 \leq 240$ (Res 2)

(d) The current optimal program is (20,40); TPBFC is $4480; TPAFC is $560.

(e) Slopes are $24, $8, and $0, with breakpoints at 160 and 320 for Resource 2. The current Resource 2 input is 160 with TPAFC of $1120.

(f) Max TPBFC $= 96X_1 + 64X_2$

Subject to: $4X_1 + 2X_2 \leq 160$ (Res 1)

   $4X_1 + 4X_2 \leq 240$ (Res 2)

   $\$4X_1 + \$8X_2 \leq \$160$ (Res 3)

(g) The new optimal program is (40,0); TPBFC is $3840; TPAFC is –$80.

(h) The financial limitation on Resource 3 forces a shift away from the efficient Process 2.

16.1 (a) The new optimal program is (16,0,0,20,4,10); TVC is $322.

(b) The cost change shifted some of the flow away from Origin 3 to Region 2 and reduced the TVC from $330 to $322.

16.2 (a) The optimal program if Origin 1 capacity is increased by 6 units is (20,2,0,20,0,14); TVC is $364.

(b) The optimal program if Origin 2 capacity is increased by 6 units is (16,0,0,26,4,10); TVC is $358.

(c) The optimal program if Origin 3 capacity is increased by 6 units is (16,0,0,20,4,16); TVC is $352.

(d) To minimize TVC, Origin 3 capacity should be increased by 6 units.

Selected Bibliography

Baumol, William J. *Economic Theory and Operations Analysis*. 3d ed. Englewood Cliffs, NJ: Prentice-Hall, 1972.

Dorfman, Robert, Paul A. Samuelson, and Robert M. Solow. *Linear Programming and Economic Analysis*. New York: McGraw-Hill, 1958.

Hillier, Frederick S., and Gerald J. Lieberman. *Introduction to Operations Research*. 2d ed. San Francisco: Holden-Day, 1974.

Koopmans, Tjalling C. *Three Essays on the State of Economic Science*. New York: McGraw-Hill, 1957.

Lancaster, Kelvin. *Introduction to Modern Microeconomics*. Chicago: Rand McNally, 1969.

Raiffa, Howard. *Decision Analysis*. Reading, MA: Addison-Wesley, 1968.

Shubik, Martin. *Game Theory and Related Approaches to Social Behavior*. New York: John Wiley, 1964.

Index

About the Author

Gerald E. Thompson received from the University of Iowa his B.A., M.A., and Ph.D degrees, which were followed by a Ford Foundation fellowship to Harvard University's Institute of Basic Mathematics for Application to Business. After many years of teaching, research, and writing, this is Professor Thompson's fourth book to be published. He has had articles published in *American Economic Review* and *Review of Economics and Statistics.*